Chr. J. Bandow

The precedents of princess Thoodamma Tsari

Chr. J. Bandow

The precedents of princess Thoodamma Tsari

ISBN/EAN: 9783337374211

Printed in Europe, USA, Canada, Australia, Japan

Cover: Foto ©ninafisch / pixelio.de

More available books at **www.hansebooks.com**

THE PRECEDENTS OF Princess Thoodamma Tsari.

TRANSLATED BY

CHR. J. BANDOW,

WITH

NUMEROUS EXPLANATORY NOTES AND

A VOCABULARY

Of the Pali and difficult Burmese words in the text.

RANGOON:
C. BENNETT, AMERICAN MISSION PRESS,
1881.

INDEX.

PREFACE.

It is a remarkable fact, that whilst all the important writings of India and Ceylon have been translated into almost every language, very few Burmese works have been so translated, notwithstanding the now acknowledged fact that Buddhism is retained in its purest from in Burmah or and that translations of Burmese MSS ought therefore to be considered as of vital importance.

The reason is, I think, not far to look for.

Burmese MSS abound in "Pali" words, for which there are in many instances no Burmese equivalents.

This in itself would not be a great drawback, but the "Pali," as written and pronounced by the Burmese, in accordance with the phonetic value of their letters, is so different from the Indo-Ceylon "Pali," that scholars who know either would not understand the other, unless acquainted also with the phonetic differences of some of the letters in both systems.

The Indo-Ceylon scholar of the "Pali" has the advantage over his Burman brother, inasmuch as he has several Pali-English dictionaries to look to for aid.

A Burma-Pali-English dictionary has never been

compiled, and as the Pali-Burmese dictionaries are not alphabetically arranged, the searching for a word is a tedious task.

In order therefore to be able to avail himself of the aid of an Indo-Ceylon-Pali-English dictionary, the scholar in Burmah is obliged to reduce the Burmese to the Indo-Ceylon rystem.

It seems almost incredible that the Burmese စကြာဝဒေး "Sakya-wadé and the Indo-Ceylon " Chackravati" (Sovereign of the four islands) are the same words. That ဇီဝ "dziva" and "jiva "—Life ; ဝိဇ္ဇာ "weidzdza" and " vijja" knowledge, သစ္စ " Thitsa" and " sachcha"—Truth, are identical—but so they are.

To be able to understand the Indo-Ceylon Pali, the Burmah scholar must know for example, that

		Burmese		*Pali*			*Burmese*		*Pali*
	စ	s.	is	ch	that	ဆ	sh	is	chh.
that	ဇ	dz	,,	j	,,	ဈ	dzh	,,	jh.
,,	တ	th	,,	th	,,	ဝ	w.	,,	v.
,,	သ	th	,,	s	,,	ဿ	thth.	,,	ss.

,, ဪ or its symbol is not pronounced aw but o.

,, the vowel a in ည is not always, and the final vowel sounds of consonants at the end of a word, are never "that" ed or killed, and in words in which two letters are written one above the other, which is equivalent to "thatting or killing the upper one, the sound of this letter is not changed, but, as in Shan and Karen, retains its inherent power; အက္ခရာ (a letter of the alphabet) for instance, would not be pronounced Ekkhara, but Akkhara; မစ္ဆာ intoxication, not Michchha, but Machchha etc:—in Indo-Ceylon Pali.

To make this work as useful as possible to students of the Burmese language, I have translated the original as literally as the preservation of the English idiom would allow of, and I have not only given a faithful rendering of the Pali words with the Pali proper in brackets, but also of many ancient Burmese words, which have now become obsolete; besides which, I have added a small vocabulary of the Pali and most difficult Burmese words in the text, which will enable the student to follow the translation, in comparing it with the original, or to make a translation for himself, without having to refer to other vocabularies or dictionaries, in which perhaps, he might not even find many of the words included in this vocabulary.

I have also added numerous notes, explaining the meaning of the religious and other technical terms in the MS which will go far, to give the reader a better understanding of the text, than he would otherwise have.

Chr. J. BANDAW.

Prome May 1881.

THOODAMMA TSARI.

(SUDAMMA CHÁRI.)

INTRODUCTION.

Glory to this Lord, (1) *venerable, complete, perfect in knowledge.*

It is said, that the words of Kings, Nobles, and Judges, as well, as those of wise men, are like the striking thunderbolt, like the sword that cuts in two the plantain leaf, and like the storm that smites the tree.

(1.) All Burmese MSS. are prefaced with the above formula, or a similar one. In some translations the word " God" is used but as Budhists do not believe in a " God," at least not in an eternal God, the creator, I have used the word "Lord" instead.

The Pali word used is "ဘဂဝ" " Bagawa; i. e. the one replete with the six glories, which are ဣဿရိယ—"Ithariya" (Issariya), Power ; ဿယ "Thaya' (Saya), splendour of attendants ; ဓမ္မ Dhamma wisdom, Righteousness, သိရိ "Thiri" (Siri), Fame, ကာမ " Kàma," the accomplishment of all desires, and ပယတ္တ "Paratta," Diligence.

The Judges who keep in mind their happiness in this and the future world, (2) do not aim at the ruin of offenders, but after examining (the case) thoroughly, decide according to the gravity or the veniality of the offence.

I. THE DISTRIBUTION OF THE THREE PUPS BETWEEN TWO DOGS.

In former times two wild dogs lived within the limits of a forest. After a long time, they increased in number by one male and two female pups. They disagreed about the apportionment of these, each taking one female pup, so that the male pup only was left.

The mother said ; "I have carried him about me in great discomfort, therefore I ought to have him."—The father said, "I, as your husband, am your lord and master, therefore it is I who ought to have him."

To settle their dispute, they went to the residence of the tiger, king (of the animals), the future Devadat. (3).

On their arrival the tiger said: "So you have come to me, have you? "Then giving one of the female pups to the father and the other to the mother, he cut the remaining male pup down the middle and gave a half to each.

---

(2). Metempsychosis, or transmigration of the soul from one body, or state of existence, into another, according to the merit or demerit of each individual, is one of the principal tenets of Buddhism.

(3). Devadat-aloung" means: Devadat that is to be, i. e. in a future existence. He became Gaudama (Gotama) Buddha's great rival and enemy, and even went to the latter with the intention of killing him, for which sin the earth opened and swallowed him. While sinking, he repented and did homage to Buddha.

When the father and the mother saw the dead body of their young one, they cried most bitterly and said: "Oh king tiger, you have certainly made a division, but is it right that you should have done it in such a cruel manner?" Then leaving the body of their young one lying before the tiger, they went away.

It is not right that kings, nobles and judges should decide as king tiger, Devadat-aloung did in the case of those two animals. Whoever does so, will fall into the four states of punishment (4.)

II. THE FOX AND THE OTTER.

In former times a fox and an otter being united in bonds of friendship went together to the banks of a river in search of food, where the otter caught a gudgeon. (5). The otter said "I wish to eat the belly and the head"! whilst the fox said, that he wished to eat them.

To settle their dispute they said let us go to the residence of our Phara-loung (6.) King Hare. King Hare

---

(4). The four states of punishment are: 1st the hells, of which there are eight stages. 2nd the state of တိရိစ္ဆာန် "Teereit-hsan (Tirichchhana)" or animals. 3rd the state of ပြိတ္တာ (Pritta) "Pyeittas," or beings, who with a mouth not larger than a needle hole and enormous stomachs, suffer the pangs of never satiated hunger. 4th the state of အသူရကာယ် "Athoorakais" (asurakaya), or beings that are dead during the day, but gain life at night. (ghosts).

(5). The spelling ငါးကြင်း in the MS. is wrong, it should be ငါးကျင်း။

(6). ဘုရားလောင်း Phaya (Bhura) loung," Buddha that is to be," i. e. Gotama in whatever state before his perfection.

said as follows: "Why are you two disputing? it is not good to terminate your friendship. Therefore, when, in future, the otter shall catch a fish, or the fox a stag or deer, always divide it as I do," and he divided the fish lengthwise from head to tail and gave them each a half, with which the fox and the otter were satisfied.

In the same manner as our embryo Buddha, king hare decided, so should Kings, Nobles and Judges decide.

A sleeping man should not be awakened.

A waking man should not be made to rise.

A sitting man should not be told to get up.

Do not be envious of another's prosperity.

The meaning of a sleeping man should not be awakened" is: "Having no selfish desires." The meaning of a waking man should not be made to rise" is: To have a desire for things, which it is lawful to desire and still not take them;" such fools will not go to the country of the Nats. (7).

---

(7). In the cosmological system of the Buddhists, the abodes of the Nats, beings superior to man, are placed above the region of the latter and consist of six stages, which are,

1st စတုမဟာရဇ် Satumaharit (Chatumaharacha); 2nd တာဝတိံသာ Tawadeintha (Tavatingsa); 3rd ယာမာ Yama; 4th တုသိတာ Tuththita (Tussita); 5th နိမ္မာနရတိ Nimmanarati and 6th ပရနိမ္မိတဝသာဝတိ Paraneimmita waththa wadi (Paranimmita vassavati.)

These Nats or Devas are called the good nats, in contradistinction to the wicked ones, who are said to inhabit the regions below the abode of man and every tree, hill, mountain, river, etc.

III. KING MAHA MANDA AND THE WATCHMAN OF THE CUCUMBER FARM.

In the life time of our Lord Waiththaphu (Vessabhu) (8). Mahā Mandá was king of the country named Parajinaka.

Marching with his army one day, the camp was pitched near the farm of a cucumber cultivator.

The king ordered his attendants to let it be known, by beat of gong, that nobody was to trespass on the cucumber farm.

At an unseasonable time of the night the king himself went out to look round, when the watchman of the cucumber-farm called out to him, "Holloa, man! don't touch the cucumbers!" and asking him what he had come there for, "Heh, man!" was the answer, "I am the king!"

The watchman who was also the owner of the ground, said "You the King! If you were, would you come here without attendants?" Then striking him with the butt of his spear in the small of the back, so that he died, left him covered with the creeping cucumber plants.

One of the ministers, knowing for certain, that the king was absent, went to the cucumber farm in search of him, when the watchman called out: "Holloa, man! do not enter the cucumber farm, just now I struck and killed a man! (for doing so), do you want to die also?"

The minister said: "Alas, for our Lord!" and, pushing the creeping plants aside, and seeing the body of the king, he reflected thus: If the army should come to know of this, it will break up; and if other kings hear

---

(8). One of the twenty eight Buddhas. He is said to have lived sixty thousand years, to have been sixty cubits in height, and to have been perfected and obtained the Buddha-ship under an အင်ကြင်း Engyin tree, (shorea robusta.) His throne is said to have occupied a space of forty cubits.

that there is no king here, they will seize and destroy our country."

He therefore said to the farmer: "Since you have killed our lord, the king, endue yourself with the dress our Lord wears, and be king in his stead!"

When the watchman heard the words of the minister, he said: "I am a poor man, why should I leave the farm on which the cucumbers grow (as numerous) as a litter of pups sucking their mother's breast, to become a king?"

The minister replied: "After you have killed our king, you refuse to act in his stead?" Then bending him down by the nape of the neck, he struck him three blows with his elbow.

On being thus struck, the watchman said, "Oh, my lord minister! do not hurt me, I will comply with your request, I cannot oppose your order, I will act as king!" So, putting the kings dress on him, the minister impressed on him that nobody would dare to raise a hand against him. They then returned to the (minister's) country.

The minister settled all in its old routine, and, on arrival, opened the white umbrella, (9.) and placed the farmer under the golden canopy. He also appointed his own son, a young man of sixteen years of age, to attend personally to the king's wants.

The queen asked the minister for information (as to all this), and, after telling her all that had occurred, she agreed to the arrangement.

At this time, the minister's son who attended the king, thought; "It is only because my father has raised him, that he has become king;" and, (in consequence he) treated him disrespectfully, on account of which the king grew sad,

---

(9). The white umbrella has always been, up to the present time, the emblem of royalty in Burmah.

saying to the youth ; "Formerly I was a poor man, and now, because your father has raised me to be a king, you treat me disrespectfully," struck him and pounded him with his elbow. (10).

The minister's son informed his father of the king's treatment of him, whereupon the father's anger rising, he said : "Is it not because I wanted this poor man to become king, that he is king ?" and intending to make use of rude language to him, went up to the palace, when the Nat-thamee, (11) presiding over the white umbrella, accosted him and said : "Hoh you minister ! this king is a king of great glory, do not use language displeasing to him !" Upon this, the two figures dwelling in the folds of the door, (12) bent him down by the nape of the neck and beat him.

The minister became excessively frightened and ashamed, and continuing steady in the good course he had taken, said : "This King is indeed very mighty ; simply because I intended to use unpleasant language towards him, this has happened to me," and raising his hands, made a most respectful obeisance to his Majesty. (13).

---

(10). A favorite mode of punishment in Burmah.

(11). The daughter of a Nat ; a devi, similar to the fairy of westerm nations. See note (7.)

(12). All the figures in the royal palace are supposed to come to life by the power of the reigning monarch and thus to assist him, in conformity with their nature, whenever he is in want of their aid. But they are also believed to turn against him, when some one more worthy of, or better entitled to the throne should come within the palace, vide ရွှေဘုံနိဒါန် Shwebong needan.

(13). The Buddhists believe implicitly, that, whatever position a man acquires, it is the result of

(We may learn from the foregoing) that to blame and speak disrespectfully, either behind their backs, or to their faces, of those who are replete with glory and power, is not proper. It is not proper for the ruler of a country to go about alone, it is because he did go alone, that this king met with his death.

A servant of a ruler should not, because he is an attendant (on the ruler), go about alone. Even a fisherman or a hunter should not go about alone.

Neither the servant of a king, nor the disciple of a priest, nor any one else, should reproach a guilty person. Why is this? Even the powerful sun and moon cannot cause the hollow of a bamboo to emit light; although the moon is powerful, in the presence of the sun she disappears. Although the asterisms and constellations are excellent, yet they have to revolve round the Myeenmho (14) mountain; although dragons are also excellent, they eat raw flesh; although the river Ganges is excellent also, it wrecks ships and boats; although wives are all that is good, yet if the slaves in the house are bad, reputation is lost.

Where are the beings that have not many sins?

---

either merit or demerit, called ကံ kan, accumulated in former existences. The minister, having been brought to consider his own position as contrasted with the kings', saw at once, that the exalted rank attained by the latter, was simply the result of merit, and that he (the minister) had been nothing more than the means of obtaining the reward of such merit. Hence his instant submission.

(14). "Myeenmho" from မြင့် high, and မိုရ် a corruption of the Meru of the Hindu mythology. It is according to Buddhist and Hindu cosmology the centre of the present system of worlds.

IV. THE RAHAN (15) KUMMARA KATHABHA AND THE THOO-HTE (16) PUNYA.

In the life time of our Lord Waththaphu (Vessabhu), the Rahan Kummara Kassabha lived in a dense forest. He was a priest of great fame.

On day he was invited by the Thoo-hte to receive offerings of food, when both the Thoo-htes wife and his daughter listened to the recitation of the law. (17).

---

(15). All the religious of the Buddhists who lead an ascetic life are called Rahans. They are generally but erroneously ealled priests; properly only those who have entered the brotherhood for good, should be called Rahans, and the novices, called ရှင် Shin, who, although they wear the yellow robe, have not yet been admitted into the fraternity, should be excluded from this title.

(16). A Thoo-hte သူဌေး is a rich man, one of the third estate, but so is a Thookywai သူကြွယ်; I therefore retain the Burmese name, as the title of the former implies some superiority over the latter. Above these are the class of Nobles, who are however only such by the kings' grace, the ministers, chiefs, etc. and above those, the royal family, in which generals, and commanders in chief are included. Below them are the various classes of merchants and the poor.

(17). The Rahans or Phoongyees are not priests, but recluses who may preperly be called monks. They perform no priestly functions and I have therefore purposely omitted to say, that Kummara Kassabha "preached." They simply recite some of the precepts of the Lord, which, although generally written in Pali, they seldom explain to their hearers.

The Rahan Kummara Kassabha made the daughter an object of his thoughts and thereby committed the sin of Nigandi. (18).

After reciting the law, he returned to the monastery and being unable to sleep, fell ill.

One day, the Thoo-hte going to invite him as before, said to him "My lord Rahan, how is it that you are ill?"

"Oh layman!" answered the Rahan, "the disposition of us Puh-tuzan (Puh-tujan) (19) is such, that if they entertain an unlawful thought of only the size of the head of a flea, they are liable to experience the troubles of common creatures, then in some way artifice is used, then the mind dwells (upon the object of thought) and (the sin of) Nigandi follows; this sin causing pleasure also causes a connection with the object of ones thoughts, steadiness in a good cause

---

(18). The Phoongyees profess to be entirely free from the desire of worldly things: The lust for the possession of gold, silver, fields, wives and children, does not dwell in our minds, we have vowed to be Rahandas, they say. The breach of this law, even in thought, is နိဂဏ္ဍိ Nigandi (contr: of နိဂဏ္ဍာဒိဒ္ဓိ Nigandadithi?) N.B. Rahandas, Pali အရိယ Ariya are beings who have entirely freed themselves from the three passions, which are the roots of all evil: desire, anger and ignorance, and lead a life of spiritual meditation.

(19). Pali ပုထုဇ္ဇနော Put-hu-zanaw (Put-hujjano) i. e. beings who are only beginning to free themselves from the passions, and have not gained the perfection of an Ariya yet. They are divided into four classes according to the proficiency they have gained viz: ဒုဂ္ဂတိအဟိတ် Doggatiaheik Duggatiahita; သုဂတ္တိအဟိတ် Phugattiaheik (Sugattiahita); ဒွိဟိတ် Dwiheik (Dvihita) and တိဟိတ် Tiheik (Tihita).

is broken, the constitution is injured, and illness is the consequence. (20).

When the Thoo-hte heard these words, and considered what object it might be, the Lord Rahan had such a desire for, he thought; The Lord Rahan was invited (to my house) and my daughter listened to the recitation of the Law, he saw her and it is she, whom he has a desire for, and if she

---

(20). Here we have a glance at Buddhist metaphysics. There are six organs of the senses: the eyes; the ears; the nose; the skin of the body; and the heart in a physical sense, [နှစ်လုံး Nhitlung in Burmese through which the heart in its moral sense, i. e. the mind, called စိတ် Seik in Burmese and မနော manaw, (Mano) in Pali], receives its inpressions. Taking the eye as an example, there is first the door အာယတန Ayatana, through which the exterior sentations are communicated to the heart, i. e. the act of seeing; 2nd the အာရုံ Ayong (Arom,) i. e. the object seen; 3rd the ဝိညာဉ် Weenyeen (Vinyana), the sense of seeing the object; 4th ဖဿ Phaththa (Phassa) i. e. the passive or active inpression it derives from the object and which it conveys to the heart. 5th ဝေဒနာ Vedana i. e. the sensation created by the impression; 6th သညာ Theenya (Sanya), i. e. the conception of the nature of the object; 7th စေတနာ Setana (Chetana) i. e. the result of such conception on the mind which is either 8th ပီတိ Piti, i. e. causing Joy; or 9th ဒုက္ခ Dukkha i. e. causing misery. 10th ဝိတက္ကံ Witekkan (Vitakkan) i. e. the dwelling or meditating of the mind on the object; 11th ဝိစာရ Wisaya (Vichàra) i. e. the consequence of such meditation; and 12th the ဓာတ် Dhat (Dháta) i. e. the constitution or physical matter, which supports the senses. The above are subdivided into 120 grades.

also loves him, I shall be put to great shame. (21) He was greatly distressed and wished that he himself might fall ill.

At that instant, the Nat-thami presiding over the Thoohtes property, created the figure of his daughter; and the Nat, presiding over the Lord Rahan's garden, created the figure of an Elephant, and in the presence of the Thoo-the and the Lord Rahan, the figure of the Elephant, with the intention of catching it, ran towards the figure of the Thoohte's daughter. She ran up to the monastery and the Elephant followed her; the damsel arrived near the Lord Rahan, the Elephant also arrived there; she then fled into a pitcher standing near, but the Elephant followed her into it. She came out by the spout, and stood near the Lord Rahan; when the Elephant followed her, his body could come out, but the tail could not, it was caught in the spout.

When the great Rahan Kummara Kassabha saw this, he said: "Oh what a wonderful occurrence is this! why does this affair happen? Oh what an event!"

Eager to know the allegory, he considerd: I have seen the representation that has taken place before me; is it not because I have coveted the beautiful damsel, that this has happened before my eyes? and to proceed in the good cause, I will now explain the simile:"

On this earth there is no aninal larger than the Elephant. Because she feared (the result of) the Elephant pursuing her, the damsel ran up to the monastery where the Elephant followed her. Because she could not evade him, she fled into the pitcher, but still the Elephant followed her

---

21. The observance of chastity is a precept which the Phoongyees strictly follow. The breach of it would never be forgiven, either by the brotherhood, or by the laity; both parties and all his connections would be irrevocably disgraced, perhaps even "stoned" and certainly excommunicated.

into it. She came running out by the spout, and, when the Elephant followed her, his body could come out of the spout but his tail could not, it was caught there!"

"As shown by this simile, the disposition of the men of the present time, although there is the comparison of "the head of a flea," (22), is, to habitually do something to the injury of all creatures!"

"Therefore the Elephant is like myself, and my unlawful desire is like the Elephant's tail, caught in the spout." (23).

The Nat-thami, who had created the figure of the Thoohte's daughter, and the Nat, who had created the Elephant, wishing that he should be mindful (of his duty) said: "Consider the consequences, in a future state, of your sin!" and the Lord Kummara Kassabha hearing these words, obtained the state of Rahanda, the moment he meditated (24) on them.

---

22. Referred to in his conversation with the Thoo-hte.

23. The explanation of the simile is, I think, this: The recluse had freed himself from all passions to such an extent, that he had accumulated a maximum of merit, comparable to the body of the Elephant, which made him very nearly ripe (as the sequel shows) for the state of Rahanda, but he was held back from obtaining that state, by that minimum of worldly passion he still retained and comparable to the Elephant's tail, which made his mind dwell on an object of unlawful desire, when he should have remained perfectly indifferent; thus, as soon as he had, by meditating on his sin, conquered that small portion of passion, he obtained the state of Rahanda.

24. "Meditation," by means of which the mind arrives at its highest possible condition, သမာဓိ Thamadhi (Samádhi), i. e. "perfect tranquility," and thus

According to this example, the Thoo-hte Punya and the reverend Kummara Kassabha are like two suitors ; the Thoo-hte's daughter is like the thing they covet.

Like the Nat-thami presiding over the Thoo-hte's property, and the Nat presiding over the garden, are those wise Judges, who decide to the thorough satisfaction of both parties.

To such Judges, it is said, the way to the abode of the Nats and to Nibpan (25) is clear.

V. THE CASE OF THE FOUR BRAHMANS.

In the lifetime of Thoomana (Sumana) (26) Buddha, one Maha Brahmana, one Meizi (Mijchy) Brahmana one Khokdik (Khuddika) Brahmana and one Sula Brahmana of the country of Thingathanago (Singassanagore), received each one hundred pieces of gold, (for goods sold).

---

emancipates itself from the sorrows and evils of life is one of the principal rules of Buddhism.

25. နိဗ္ဗာန် "Neikban," properly နိဗ္ဗာနံ "Nibbana" in Pali, "Nirvanna" in Sanscrit, is generally understood to be "total annihilation," or "destruction," but there is something defective in this definition. The etymology of the word is "to go out" (as a fire or light) so that there is nothing "active," in the idea of the word, but something rather "passive." It thus signifies "the end" (of existence) i. e. the deliverance from any future birth.

26. One of the twenty eight Buddhas. He is said to have lived ninety thousand years, and to have been ninety cubits high ; was perfected and obtained the Buddha ship under a ကံကော် or ကဂေါ် "Kangaw". Mesua tree. There is very little on record about him.

On going home they had occasion to take a bath and said: "Let us put all our money (27) together."

The three elder Brahmans accordingly did so, but the youngest intending to deceive, hid his money elsewhere, thinking that thus the money of the (other) three would have to be divided among them and him. He pretended therefore to place his money with theirs, and then they all bathed together.

When the four came out of the water together, the money of the three (eldest) Brahmans being where they had placed it, and that of the youngest not, the latter said: "Brother Brahmans, my money has disappeared (from where it was,) why should yours be there? Will you (not) give me (some of yours?") They replied; "Nobody has come to this place, if your property has disappeared from where it was placed by us four, for what reason should we give you (a share)?" and disputing with each other, they went to the Judge of the town, to abide by his decision.

The Judge said; "It is not right that the money of one (of you) should disappear out of that placed together by you four," and decided that they should divide equally.

The three Brahmans repudiated their liability to a division, and went to the governor of the town, who sent them to the minister, who in turn sent them to the king of the country.

The king said, that the decision of the Judge of the town was just, but the three Brahmans were dissatisfied and

---

27. The word used in the original is ඉඩං Ussa (Uchchá) which means "any property" or "goods," but as this word is not always appropriate, I have made use of more suitable words, throughout this work.

said so, whereupon the king made the minister responsible and said: "Heh, you minister! you decide this case within seven days, if you do not, I will confiscate your property!"

The minister, in great fear, called together the four Brahmans, and, although he made a searching enquiry, he could not form an opinion and became greatly distressed. At this time his beloved daughter, named Sanda Kummari, seeing her father's sad countenance, said to him: "Oh, honored father! why are you so distressed?"

"Oh my beloved daughter!" he replied, "I am held responsible to decide the case of these four Brahmans in seven days, if I do not, I am very much afraid, my property will be confiscated.

"Do not be troubled, dear father" she said, "I will find out the thief, only build a large Mandat." (28)

After the minister had done what his daughter wanted she placed the four Brahmans at the corners inside the mandat and sitting down herself in the middle, asked them to tell her of the Eighteen Sciences, (29) such as the art of observation, the proverbs of common life, logic, philosophy,

---

28. A temporary shed raised on every festive occasion, and got up in a more or less costly manner, according to the circumstances of the builder.

29. Pali အဋ္ဌာရသ Athayatha (Athárasa), consisting of the following:

1st. အကြားအမြင် Akya-Amyeen, literally; hearing and seeing; i. e. the art of observation or acquiring experience without tuition.

2nd. ဓမ္မသတ် Dhammathat (Dhammasata), i. e. the Law.

3rd. ဂဏန်းအတတ် Ganan-atat, i. e. arithmetic.

4th. တံစဉ်းရူးဆောက်စသောအတတ် literally the science of the adz, awl and chisel, and such like, i. e. carpentrv.

magic, the law of poetry, a little from pharmacy, and the five treatises on diseases." "I wish to hear what you know of these!" she said. "Oh, Lady!" they answered, "we are unable to do this," and on being asked the reason, they replied: "On our way (home), not one of us could tell which of us would act dishonestly, but the (good) practices of us Brahmans have been put to great shame; this is the reason why we are unable, but you, Lady Sanda Kummari," they said, "being constantly near the great minister, you will have acquired much experience by listening to the enquiries made from all quarters, please say

---

5th. နီတိကျမ်းအတတ် Nitikyam, i. e. the book of proverbs, of which there are three kinds, viz: ဓမ္မနီတိ Dhamma Niti-proverbs, pertaining to religion,

လောကနီတိ Lawka (Loka) Niti proverbs pertaining to common life, and ရာဇနီတိ Raza (Raja) Niti-proverbs pertaining to Government.

6th. ဗျာကရိုဏ်း Byakaraing (Bya Karana), the art of interpreting omens.

7th. စောင်းညှင်းစသော အတတ် Soung, Nhyeeng sa thaw atat, i. e. the art of playing instruments like the harp, trumpet, etc. music.

8th. လက်ပစ်အတတ် Letpit atat, i. e. the art of manual offence and defence.

9th. ဒူးလေးလင်းလေးစသောအတတ် Doolé, Linlé sa thaw atat, literally the bow, crossbow and such like, i. e. archery.

10th. စကားဟောင်းပုံပြင်အတတ် Saga houng pong pyeeng-atat, i. e. the art of adapting old sayings. The Pali word used is ပုရဏာ Purana, which refers to none other than the Hindu Puranas, and which treat of theogonies, accounts of the creation, philosophical speculations, instructions for religious ceremonies, fragments of history and legends, relating to the actions of devas, heroes and sages.

something for us to note!" "Oh! "said she, I do not know any of the sayings of you teachers, (30) but if you will allow me to relate to you an allegory, I will do so."

The Prince, the Nobleman's son, the son of a commoner and the Thoohte's daughter.

Once upon a time, when a Nobleman's son, the son of a commoner and a Thoo-hte's daughter were learning the sciences (31) the latter retained in her memory all that the teacher taught.

11th. ဆေးအတတ် Hsai atat; i. e. medicine.

12th. ရယ်ရွှင်မှုအတတ် Yai shwing mhoo atat, i. e. comicry, wit.

13th. ဗေဒင်အတတ် Baiding-atat, i. e. the Vedas, which are said to have been written by ten hermits and of which there were four books, but one was lost; the three remaining are သာမ Thama (Sàma) ယဇု Yazoo (yaju) and ဣသျှု Eeshoo.

14th. လှည့်ပတ်တတ်သောအတတ် Hlai pat tat thaw atat, i. e. Legerdemain.

15th. ဆန်းကျမ်းအတတ် Hsan kyan atat, i. e. composition, (of writings.)

16th. သံတမန်အတတ် Than taman atat, i. e. Diplomacy.

17th. မန္တာန်အတတ် Mantan atat, i. e. making charms and philters.

18th. သဒ္ဒါကျမ်းအတတ် Thadda kyam atat, i. e. Grammar.

(30). The Brahmans are even now considered by the Burmese as very learned in all sciences, chiefly in the Vedas and astronomy. The astrologers employed at the Court of Ava are Brahmans.

(31). တက္ကသိုလ် in Burmo-Pali is Tekkatho, a corruption of the Pali proper of တက္ကသီလ Takkasila.

Once she dropped her style, and, seeing the Prince below, requested him to hand it up to her.

He said "If you tell me to hand it up to you, I will do so, but I want you to make me a promise; when we arrive at our native town, will you come and give me your virgin love?" and he did not hand her the style, until she had promised that she would (so go to him).

When she had become skilled in the sciences, she returned home, and the Prince also returned.

His father died, and he succeeded to the throne. The Thoo-hte's daughter having arrived at the age of sixteen years, was given in marriage by her parents to a suitable man.

Then she entreated her husband thus: "I have become your wife, please give me permission to go (out) for a while!"

He asked her, why she wished to go out.

"Because" she said, "when learning the sciences at Taxila, I made a promise; the Prince told me that when I returned to my parents, I should first come to him, and I promised him that I would."

Although one may have been given in marriage by parents, the sacredness of a promise is very great, both among the religious and the laymen, therefore her husband said that he would give her permission; so after rubbing his feet with her hair, he being her lord and master, (32) she dressed and adorned herself.

---

(32). In the Manoo Dammathat or Laws of Manoo Chapter V. Section XXI it says; If the wife makes religious offerings without her husband's knowledge, she has no right to do so, the merit she ought to obtain will not be much. If the husband makes religious offerings, without the knowledge of

Going away she met a thief who caught hold of her arm firmly and said: "Where are you going to? what impropriety for a woman to go about like this! either your life or your ornaments are mine! what is your intention?"

"It is true they are yours," she answered, "as to why I am going about, it is thus: when I learned the sciences at Taxila, the Prince told me to go to him first on my return to my own country, and I engaged to do so, therefore if I break my promise, I shall fall into the four states of punishment and shall not arrive at the abode of the good; (for this reason) I have asked permission of the husband to whom my parents have given me in marriage (33) and have come away.

---

his wife, or offerings of affection to other people, he has a right to do so, and the wife also obtains merit. The wife has no right to object to offerings of the husband, but he may object to those of the wife; this is *because the husband is the lord of the wife.* In Chapter VIII Section III, it says: If the husband without the knowledge of his wife small make a present to another of a portion of the property common to both, and the receiver be not his lesser wife, let it be kept as it was given, the wife shall not say "it is our joint property, I did not know (of the gift);" she shall not take it back, why is this: *because the husband is the lord of the wife.*

(33.) In Burmah there are three ways of becoming man and wife, viz:

1st A man and woman given in marriage by their parents.

2nd A man and woman brought together by the intervention of a go-between.

3rd A man and woman who come together by mutual consent, but it is requisite in all three cases

The thief when he heard these words, said ; "When you keep your promise to the prince, also keep this one. On your return home you must call at my place!" and released her.

After being freed by the thief, she went on and arrived at a Banyan tree and the Nat presiding over the Banyan tree asked her where she was going.

She said : "Oh, Lord Nat presiding over the Banyan tree, I have arrived at your place for no other purpose than this," and she repeated what she had said before.

He said "keep this promise just as you keep that to the prince : On your return call at my place!" and let her go.

She arrived at the prince's palace and because she kept her faith in her engagement, the Nat watching over the palace, opened the door.

When she arrived before the king, he asked her why she had come. "Oh, great king! she said," (I am) the young lady who made you a promise, when learning the sciences at Taxila. I have removed from thence and have been given in marriage by my parents. Having asked permission from the master of the house, my husband, I have come into your Majesty's presence."

The prince said : "This is very wonderful! verily, you have kept your promise!" and after praising her and saying that he would make her offerings of many valuables, he did so and let her go.

She accepted all the valuable presents and going away, encountered the Nat presiding over the Banyan tree, when

---

that they should live and eat together, and the first of these is looked upon as the most respectable. Hence the young lady's allusion to the fact of having been thus married.

with the voice of the Karaweik, (34) she said: "Oh Lord Nat of the Banyan tree! are you sleeping or are you awake? I have redeemed my promise to the prince and have returned; my life is yours, Oh, Lord Nat of the Banyan tree! I have not broken my promise, and I have arrived at your dwelling!

The Nat, when he heard the young lady's voice, said, "Young lady, a person has been freed from the hands of an enemy, and thus his life is safe, he, whose life has thus been saved returns again to the (aforesaid) enemy to die; how is this possible?"

"Oh, Lord Nat of the Banyan tree!" she replied, "if I had broken my promise for fear of my life and had gone on without calling here, I should have fallen into the four states of punishment, and should never arrive at the abode of the blessed."

The Nat made an offering of a pot of gold to the young lady for her integrity and, telling her, that it would last her for the whole of her life, he let her go.

The young lady leaving the Banyan tree arrived at the thief's abode, who already was sleeping.

Although by going on, while he was asleep, she would have been safe, she called out: "Oh master thief!" and rousing him said: "Either my life or the things I have with me are yours, I have arrived on account of my promise, I will not oppose your desire!" The thief said: "How wonderful! You really do keep faith, a thing rare in this world; if I should sin against such a person, I should have to suffer great misery, go away quick!" and let her go.

---

(34) A fabulous bird said to possess a very sweet voice.

"When she arrived at her husband's, she told him all that had happened and having told him all about the thief, the Nat of the Banyan tree and the prince, her husband praised her for what she had done.

Having finished, the young Lady Sanda Kummari asked the Brahmans, whom, in the tale she had just told them, they thought most worthy of praise.

The eldest Brahmin said: "Oh, daughter of the great minister; I praise the prince! For what reason? Because he rejected the young lady's first love which was proffered him, and this is in accordance with the ten kingly virtues; (35) this is something to be wondered at, therefore I praise it.

Another Brahman said: "Oh, daughter of the great minister! I praise the Nat presiding over the Banyan tree; for what reason? Because this dryad not only restrained his desires, which is very difficult for even men to do, but he also gave a present of a pot of gold, and as this is very wonderful, I praise him!"

Another Brahman said: "Oh daughter of the great minister, I praise the husband; he is like the water in

---

(35) မင်းကျင့်ရာသောတရားဆယ်ပါး။ The ten kingly virtues or duties are:

1st အလှူပေးခြင်း "Ahloo-pe-gyin," To make religious offerings; 2nd သီလ Thila (Sila) ဆောက်တည်ခြင်း။ To perform the religious duties; 3rd စွန့်ကြဲပေးကမ်းခြင်း။ To give away in charity; 4th ဖြောင့်မတ်ခြင်း To be righteous, just; 5th စိတ်နှလုံးနူးညံ့ခြင်း To be gentle (of gentle character); 6th အမျက်နည်းခြင်း literally to have little anger, i.e. to be good-tempered; 7th ခြိုးခြံစွာကျင့်ခြင်း To practice self-denial; 8th သည်းခံခြင်း To be forgiving; 9th သူ့အားမညှဉ်းဆဲခြင်း Not to be oppressive; and 10th ပြည်တောင်းမင်းတို့ကိုမပျက်စီးခြင်း Not to destroy or ruin (other) countries and kings.

which a pure ruby has been cleansed; when his wife asked him for permission, he allowed her to go, that man's disposition is a most wonderful one, therefore I praise him!"

The youngest Brahman said: "Oh, daughter of the great minister! I praise the thief; for what reason? A thief supports himself by risking his life, and a person who thus supports himself, did not covet the dress and ornaments, but abstained from taking them; nor did he covet the gold and silver, but abstained from taking them too; that thief is praisworthy, I laud and praise him!"

A young lady, an attendant of the minister's daughter, said: "The master's daughter, the three (elder) Brahmans and myself respectively praise either the prince, the Nat of the Banyan tree, or the husband, but the youngest Brahman praises the thief!"

When the minister's daughter heard this, she said to her attendant: "The admission of the youngest of the four Brahmans, that he thinks the thief who did not covet the things he might have taken, but abstained from taking, is the most excellent, shews, that he is in possession of the (missing) property; this being so, you, my sister, personate me and go to the younger Brahman and say to him: I come for no other purpose but this, the words of the three Brahmans being those of fools, and you, the youngest, being a wise man, I have come to become your spouse; (36) what is to be done, that you and I may live together? I am afraid of my father, and you have lost the property you had; I am empty handed, if you and I go to another place, we have nothing to live upon."

---

(36) An old Indian custom, in accordance with which princesses and maidens of the highest caste were allowed to select their own husbands. See "Nala and Damajanti" and "Narada's prediction" in the Mahabbharata.

Having arranged thus, she let her attendant go. When the Brahman saw her, he accosted her, and the attendant spoke to him as (she had been) instructed to do.

When he heard what she said, he was very glad and replied: "Oh, young Lady! do not be troubled, the property is not lost, it is in my possession, I only acted like this, to get a share; there is sufficient to live on; even if we go to another place, there is enough."

The attendant informed her mistress of what the Brahmin had told her.

The minister's daughter went to her father and told him, that the (missing) property was in possession of the youngest Brahman, adding: "If you give me a sum equal to the (lost) amount, I can recover the latter." So the minister gave his daughter what she wanted.

She gave the money to the attendant and instructed her (what to do,) and then said: "Now my sister, go and stay with the Brahman, show him this money and say as you have been instructed."

The attendant showed the Brahman the money and requested him to show her his, saying, in accordance with her instructions: "I have only a little money with me, but putting yours and mine together, we shall be able to live upon it, even if we go to another place," upon which the Brahman gave her his money.

The attendant, when she had obtained possession of the money gave it to the minister's daughter, who greatly rejoiced, said: "Now, my sister, go to the other three Brahmans and ask for (their money) in this manner: "You three Sirs, give me your money for awhile, I will put it in a certain place, and you go and petition the King, when all four of you will be satisfied."

It being asked for in this manner, the three elder

Brahmans said: "very well!" and in accordance with the lady's request, gave (her) the three sums of money.

The young lady then informed her father, that she was in possession of the money of all the four Brahmans, and the minister reported to the King that the (combined) money of the four Brahmans had been obtained.

When the King asked by what manner of investigation it had been obtained, the minister said; "My daughter inquired (into the matter) and obtained it."

The King called for the young lady and the four Brahmans and questioned her, when she said: "This is a fearful case, much artifice has been resorted to! The Brahmans are wise men! we mortals are by nature the slaves of cupidity, anger and ignorance; I will give an instance: "the ear seduces the eye, the eye seduces the mind, thus worldly desires are created, prudence is lost, and then without reflection, a bad deed is apt to be done, the consequence of which is the suffering of misery in a future state."

After these words the young lady said: "I have placed your four portions before the King, take what you own;" and the Brahmans took their property.

After three portions had been taken, the youngest Brahman took the remaining portion, when the King said: "Although it has been said, that some money has been lost, how is it, that the youngest Brahman's money is there now?"

"Oh, Sire!" said the minister's daughter, "he had hidden his money, but now he himself has pointed it out, therefore the money of the four Brahmans has been recovered!" upon which the Fairy (Nat-thamee) presiding over the King's umbrella called out, "Well done."

And the King, (considering) that the young lady was full of wisdom and able to examine into and solve all subects under discussion with ambassadors from all foreign ountries, he made her his chief Queen.

Therefore Judges should take example from this and decide (cases) with due consideration.

VI. THE CASE OF THE THOO-HTE'S SON, THE THOO-HTE'S DAUGHTER AND THE YOUNG MAN PETA.

In the lifetime of our Lord Thoomedha (37) (Sumedha) in the country of Ketumati, the son of a man possessing untold wealth, and a Thoo-hte's daughter named Thawga (Soga) were given to each other in marriage by their respective parents.

On one occassion the Thoo-hte's son said: "Our parents have a great deal of property but we have none, therefore I will go on board ship and go with other men to the island of Sanda!"

The Thoo-hte's daughter, his wife, said to her consort: "If you go away trading, I have no one to trust to; only destitute people cross the ocean, and as your parents and mine possess untold wealth, do not go!" thus she entreated him in affectionate terms.

When he heard this speech of his wife, the Thoo-hte's son said: "It is excellent to have property obtained by diligence; it is excellent to be diligent even if one should

---

(37) One of the twenty-eight Buddhas. He is said to have attained the age of Ninety thousand years, and to have been Eighty cubits high. He went into solitude on the back of an Elephant, practised self denial for Eight months, and was perfected and obtained his Buddha-ship under a တမာပင် Tamà or Tragecanth tree.

die in the sea ; a man who has no property is depraved ; he ought to be ashamed, their way of living also is mean, therefore it has been said by wise men, that those who wishing to obtain property, risk their lives on the ocean, are worthy of praise, even though they may not obtain (property), so I shall go," and taking stock in trade he left.

The young man Peta and the Thoo-hte's daughter cohabited, and Peta said: "We live together now, but how can we do so, when your husband returns ?" (38).

The Thoo-hte's daughter suggested to him, that if a corpse were brought from the burial ground and placed in the Pyathat (39) and then fire be set to the latter, the corpse would be consumed. " It will be said that the Thoo-hte's daughter was burned to death and we two will go to another place and live there," she said, and in accordance with her suggestion (he) brought a corpse up to the house and after having set fire to it, they went to another place.

The parents thinking that (their daughter) was really burnt, (to death) burned the corpse by cremation with much weeping and wailing.

Peta and the Thoo-hte's daughter lived at another place. There was no food at that place: "we are very miserable here," said the Thoo-htes daughter, " going back to our place, my parents will see me and say, " Oh, how

---

(38). According to para 16 of the 5th vol. of the Institutes of Menu a woman must wait three years for the return of her first husband before she has a right to take another husband, this young lady evidently did not wait so long.

(39). The word used in the original ပြာသာဒ် Pyathat, means a graduated turret surmounting the roof of palaces, monasteries etc: in which, in Burmah, there are no rooms or chambers, so for want of a better word I have retained the original one.

very like our danghter!" they will give us presents and thus we shall get food"; so they went and arrived at the tank in the parent's garden. Whilst they were resting there under the shade of a flowering tree, the Thoo-hte's young men came to draw water in place of the Thoohte's daughter, to sprinkle the flower-vases with, and seeing her they said, "If it was not for this young lady's having a consort, we should say that she is really our master's daughter," and taking the golden vases returned to the house.

The young men told the Thoo-hte's wife what they had seen, and when she herself went and looked and saw her daughter, she wept bitterly and on asking, was told that they were travellers and would have to go on presently.

The Thoo-hte's wife said: "Oh, do not go, I will adopt you as my daughter;" and took them to the house and placed them in the Pyathat.

Then the first husband, the Thoo-hte's son, arrived and enquired after his wife. Hearing that she was burnt with the Pyathat, he weeping bitterly went into the Pyathat built by the mother, to look, and seeing his wife there said, "Why is it said, that my wife is dead, when she is there?" and petitioned the Judge of the town; but as his mother in law and many people said, that his wife had been burnt to death, in the Pyathat, he lost (his case).

Being dissatisfied he went to the Governor, but lost again.

He then went to the king, who being artless in law matters, the fairy presiding over the white umbrella, said: "Oh, great king! this is not a case for an ignorant person; is not your majesty's minister skilful in the decision of lawsuits?"

When he heard this, he called the minister and said,

"Hai, you minister! decide this case, or your property will be confiscated."

The minister was very sad, and his daughter seeing this, asked him; "Oh my father why are you downcast?"

The minister told her of the royal order, when she said: "Do not be distressed, Oh my father! but let all three come to me, let a building be erected and let the three sit in three corners separate, and I will sit in the middle and inquire into (the case") Having thus arranged, she called the Thoohtes son, and said: "Oh, excellent man of glorious reputation! After you, my brother, have risked your life in crossing the ocean and in search of wealth, every one says, that your wife was burnt, together with the steeple; and although, my brother, your parents are very rich, you have crossed the Ocean and you have acquired much property; for such an one to contend with another man about a woman, is not proper! and because the young lady says, that she is his wife, and he, that she is his wife, both the Judge and the Governor have decided against you. If, my brother, she is really your wife, why should she deny it? You, my brother, ought to concur with my opinion. What will you my brother, think; and how am I to say it?"

"What are you going to say?" asked the Thoo-hte's son in return.

She said: "Oh, my brother, I am the minister's daughter, if we two are of one mind we should be happy for the whole of our lives." (40).

---

(40). It must be borne in mind by the readers, that there is nothing indelicate in the young lady's thus offering herself as the young merchant's wife, as it was a custom in ancient India for young ladies to select their own husbands, vide Note 35, moreover it was all pretention in this case, as the young lady wanted to find out the two young men's character.

The Thoo-hte's son replied: "How can I forsake this my wife, who was betrothed to me by our parents before she cut her (second ?) teeth, even before she was able to put on her own clothes (for herself.) The man (of such a wife) ought not to do any thing unfeeling and harsh; what would be the advantage of breaking faith ?"

"It is something wonderful to hear the words of a man, who is so loyal" she said, and sent him away.

Then she accosted the young man Peta and said: "You are an excellent man and of great reputation, and it is not proper that you two young men should quarrel about one woman! I have no consort my wish is to live with you, we shall be much respected, besides I am the daughter of the great minister, shall we not enjoy much comfort ?"

When Peta heard this, he thought to himself: This is a wise person; it is in the nature of women to have many expedients; they know how to deceive and to conceal; and my life is like water in the hollow of this young lady's hand, therefore, (he said) "I will comply with my Lady's words."

"If my brother will do so," she replied, we must go and live at some other place, only then will I trust you. He agreed to this; when she exclaimed, "for the present retire," and he left her.

After this she called the Thoo-hte's daughter and asked her: "Your husband, my sister, has but little, while the Thoo-hte's son is very wealthy; by living with him you would never be in want during the whole of your life, why do make objections ?"

"You my lady," she replied, "are a woman, and so am I; we women are like the fruit of a tree; that husband who is my lord, is like the tree; the nature of fruits is this: a young shoot sprouts out and two leaves grow on it, one above the other, the stalk of the leaves forms a bud, from the bud comes a flower and from the flower the fruit, the fruit ripens and when ripe, it falls off, when fallen it remains where it falls; does the fallen fruit re-attach itself to the stalk? does the born babe re-enter its mother's womb?"

When the minister's daughter heard the words of the Thoo-hte's daughter, she thought to herself; "Now I know the dubious position of this woman," and telling the three litigants to return to their respective dwellings, they left, when she caused a secretary to record every thing she had been told by and had heard from the three, and had it read to her father. He was very glad and calling the three parties before the King, they on being asked, acknowledged (the record) to be correct.

The King decided: "That the young man Peta, not being the husband, ought to die, but that he would pardon him; that the merchant prince, the Thoo-hte's son, although possessing great riches, had not broken his troth, and that he was the real husband; that the Thoo-hte's daughter, on account of having disowned her husband, had cited the maxims: "that a ripe fruit having fallen from its stalk, does not re-attach itself to the same; and that a born babe does not re-enter its mother's womb," wherefore she should be castigated and set free."

Upon this, the fairy presiding over the white umbrella gave praise, and the King raised the minister's daughter to be his Queen.

For this reason, wise Judges should decide cases of a deceitful and dubious character after examining and sifting them.

VIII. THE CASE OF THE SHIP-OWNER AND THE GOAT-HERD.

Once upon a time a Ship-owner going on a trading voyage, arrived at the opposite shore of the ocean. On the beach was a man herding many goats, and the Ship-owner's she-goat went after a he-goat (among them.) He demanded his she-goat from the owner of the he-goat, and on the refusal of the latter, went to the Judge to make his claim.

The decision was, that because the she-goat had gone after the he-goat, she should be forfeited, the he-goat had a right to her.

After this decision, the Ship-owner being dissatisfied, sent to the Judge's daughter with presents, and after so sending many times, she went to the Ship-owner's place. She was kept there and not allowed to return.

The Judge demanded his daughter but was refused.

A dispute arising, the Ship-owner, going to the king, said: "Oh, great king, recently my she-goat followed a he-goat, and on referring to the Judge, he himself decided that the owner of the he-goat had a right to her; Now this Judge's daughter has come to my place, so I have a right to her."

In accordance with this former plea, the Ship-owner acquired a right to the Judge's daughter. Therefore if a woman go to a man, he is free from guilt.

IX. THE CASE OF THE PASSIONATE YOUNG LADY RATTEE EETHARI.

In the life-time of our Lord Koukkathan a young lady named Rattee Eethari lived in a small town. One day, being in a great rage with her husband, she went to another town.

As the distance was great she became fatigued and rested under the shade of a Palm-tree, and thinking that her child would sleep, while she rested, she spread her shawl and put the child to sleep upon it.

A crow came flying along and perched upon a palm-fruit, which fell on the child's head and killed it.

Seeing the child dead, she wept, and taking the corpse in her arms, followed in the direction in which the crow was flying.

As the crow had eaten every day the bundle of rice which a ploughman used to place on the ridge of the paddy field, the crow was caught in the trap which the ploughman had laid; the latter came to take the crow and called out: "Ah, this crow is mine!"

"If that crow is your's," said the dead child's mother, "is it proper that he should kill my son?" And a dispute arising between them, they went to a Judge who was not very wise, and who decided, that the man ought to give compensation to the woman for the loss of her child.

The ploughman being dissatisfied went to a reputedly wise Judge, who decided as follows:

Because you quarrelled with your husband, you went to another village, and the distance being great, you rested under the shade of a palm-tree; you put the child to sleep and whilst it slept, a palm-fruit fell on it and killed it.

Your quarreling with your husband is the cause of the child's death ; therefore get another son by the ploughman, and when you have got that son, give him to your husband.

X. THE CASE OF THE FOOLISH BRAHMAN AND THE WILD DOG.

Formerly, in the life time of our Lord Thoomana there lived in the country of Girikama, a Brahman named Adimanda.

Every night a wild dog came into the town and ate the bones and scraps that had been thrown away.

Early in the morning, being afraid, he used to return to the jangal.

Once, the Brahman Adimanda went among the bushes for the purpose of purification and seeing a wild dog, took up a stick. The dog being frightened said: "Oh my Lord Brahman; what would be the good of killing me? Do not kill me and I will give you two thousand (viss of) gold."

When the Brahman heard this, he, longing for wealth said: "I will not kill you, but give me what you have said that you would."

"Oh, my Lord Brahman! how can I get it here? if you carry me to my place, then I can give it to you," replied the dog.

"Halloa you dog!" said the Brahman, "you are a creature of the jangal, it is not becoming that I should carry you."

"If my lord says so," replied the dog, "then by making a cradle of your putsoe, and carrying me in it over the shoulder, people who see it, will think it is your offspring."

The Brahman coveting the money, said ; "I agree with what you say ;" and carried the dog away in the manner the dog had suggested.

On arriving at the dog's place, he said : "Oh, my lord Brahman," I owe you much gratitude for not killing me, please wait till sunset for me, to bring you the two-thousand (viss of) gold ;" saying which he went into the jangal.

The Brahman, poor fellow, waited the whole day, and a traveller seeing him, asked : "Oh Brahman, what are you waiting for ?" and the Brahman related all that the dog had said.

After listening, the traveller thought to himself, this Brahman is a great deal more stupid, than the dog, and said: "How can you believe the words of a dog, that cannot even find food for himself ? go back home."

Only then the Brahman returned.

Therefore, the disposition of wise men is, not to trust those whom it is inconsistent to trust. One ought to consider. Whoever believes words that should not be believed will be like the Brahman, who was deceived by the dog.

XI. THE CASE OF THE THREE MEN WHO LOST THEIR LIVES BY ASSOCIATING WITH AN IMPROPER PERSON.

Once upon a time, the son of a nobleman the son of a Thoo-hte and a prince, were learning the sciences at Taxila. One of them learned the attributes of bones ; one, those of matter, and the third those of the spirit.

Having learned these, they returned to their own country, when, in the cover of a jangal, they found the bones of a tiger.

They thought : by putting these bones together, we shall get the figure of the tiger, then by putting breath into it, it will become a live tiger, that will go with us, and when he kills Rusa-deer, Barking-deer, wild Oxen and Elks, we shall eat them; then also if we should meet with enemies, the tiger will keep them off, and we shall be safe.

So the one who understood the atributes of bones, joined them together properly; the one, who understood the atributes of matter, formed the figure of the tiger; and the one who understood the atributes of the spirit, put breath (life) into it, and the tiger being thus brought to life, followed them.

From the jaugal they cames to the open plain and all three went to sleep under a Banyan tree.

As there was no prey for the tiger in the open plain, he being very hungry devoured one out of the three and carried the bones away somewhere else.

When the other two awoke, they said; "Hollo, tiger! one of us has disappeared and is avoiding us, so only you and we are left, if we get any venison, there will be only us three to share it."

On arriving at another halting place he devoured another one.

The remaining one said: "One more of us has disappeared, if we get elk and deer, you and I only shall eat them."

On arriving at a thick forest, he devoured the last man.

Thus all three young men came by their death.

So one should be prudent and not associate with improper persons.

XII. THE CASE OF THE HIGHMINDED THOO-HTE AND THE BARBER.

In the life time of our Lord Maidingya (41) a certain Thoo-hte went on a journey with his wife.

One night meeting a Barber on the road, the Thoo-hte moved out of his way.

When the Barber saw the Thoo-hte get out of his way, he said: "It is I who should yield the road, why are you doing so?" and gave the Thoo-hte a slap in the face.

The Thoo-hte, being very much ashamed and greatly concerned that others might hear of this, was very sad at heart.

Other Thoo-hte's talked to each other about this, so that in due course the king heard about it, and calling the Thoo-hte, questioned him, but the latter kept silent.

After asking two or three times, the king said; "It is true what the people say."

Calling the Barber and asking him, the latter admited it to be true and said,

"It is because he moved out of the way, when it was I who should have done so, that I slapped his face."

The Thoo-hte was unable to say a word, and from very shame sat with his back turned.

The king gave the Barber over to the executioners and ordered them to cut his hands and feet off and to set him adrift on a raft, (42.)

(41.) One of the twenty eight Buddhas, who is said to have attained the age of ninety thousand years, and was perfected under a ပေါက်ပင်။ Poukbing, Butea.

(42.) This was a very common punishment in India. There are several dzats or dramas in Burmah

When the Thoo-hte heard this sentence he gave the executioners a piece of gold and said to them; neither cut the Barber's hands and feet off, nor set (him) adrift on a raft."

When the executioners heard his words, they reported them to the king.

The king called the Thoo-hte and said to him: Why have you said, do not execute (the Barber)? "Oh great king" answered the Thoo-hte "Let the Barber put me to shame in this country only! If he is fastened to a raft and set adrift, at whatever place the raft grounds, he will be asked, why he has been set adrift and he will say: "Because when I should have got out of the way, a Thoo-hte did so instead, so I slapped his face." Then he will be told that he is a very irascible man and not fit for their country and being set afloat again, it will be known every where. How can that be good?"

When the king heard these words, he gave the Thoo-hte a great many presents.

The Thoo-hte (thought to himself) it is because the Barber slapped my face that I get all this property and gave the Barber (some of it); and only then did the Thoo-hte wash his head (43.)

For this reason wise man should not talk of what they see secretly. One should not act ostentatiously as to any thing, so that others get to hear (of it). It is said, that although offenders may not be blamed, still they suffer in some way or other for their offences.

---

in which the offenders are represented as suffering this purnishment. Vide Weezaya dzat, Padongma dzat, etc.

(43.) By way of purification from the polluting touch of the low-caste Barber.

XIII. THE CASE OF THE IRRITABLE POTTER AND THE WASHERMAN.

In the life time of our Lord Thoomaida, a Potter, being bent on evil designs, because he saw with envy, the increasing prosperity of a neighbouring washerman, who, with a large establishment of dependants, cleansed clothes, committed a great error.

He addressed the King thus: "Your Majesty has a royal Elephant, which is black; to make him white, order my neighbour, the Washerman, to wash him; will you not then be Lord of the white Elephant?"

He did not thus address the King from a desire to benefit him, but because he thought, that if the washerman was ordered to wash the Elephant, and he could not make him white, he would be ruined, and because he wished him to be ruined, he thus petitioned the King.

The King when he heard what the Potter said thought that it could really be done, and having little wisdom, he, without consideration called the washerman, and said: "Heh, you washerman! you wash my Elephant white!"

The washerman knowing the potter's design, addressed the King thus: "Oh, great King! the business of a washerman is to wash clothes white by means of steam and soap, and beating them, and your Majesty's royal Elephant can only become white by being steamed and beaten in the same manner, therefore only by my putting the Elephant in a suitable perforated vessel and steaming him, can I wash him white."

When the King heard these words, he said: "Pots and vessels are not a matter for washermen, they concern potters;" and calling the potter said: "Heh, you potter!

as he must be steamed with soap and water in a large steaming pot, you must make a suitable one for my Elephant!"

When he heard the King's word, he called all his relatives together, heaped up a mass of clay and made a vessel suitable for the Elephant to be steamed in, and took it to the King.

The King called the washerman and gave the vessel to him.

When the soap had been put in, the Elephant stepped into the vessel, which broke; and when another stronger one was made (the water) would not boil, because it was too thick; if it was too thin again, the Elephant on putting only his foot into it, broke it.

So as he had to do it over again many times, the potter could not make a living and was ruined.

So whoever plans the ruin of others, is said, not to plan the ruin of others, but his own. Although having little property one should not scheme against others. One should always avoid those, who resort to tricks.

XIV. THE CASE OF THE BRAHMAN AND HIS WIFE AND DAUGHTER.

In the lifetime of our Lord Ta-hnin-gaya (44) the Brahman Oodeissa (Udichcha) was the owner of ten million worth of property and had but one only and beloved daughter, named Thamodda Seitta Kongmari (Samudda Sitta Kummari.) When she arrived at the age of fifteen, she had learned prudence and thought to herself: "my parents

---

(44). One of the twenty-eight Buddhas who is said to have attained the age of eighty thousand years and was perfected under a စရည်ပင် Sayeebing, for which I cannot find the English equivalent name.

have only me; they do not love me; because they are very parsimoneous, they give me nothing, although they are rich.

When they shall be summoned by the king of terrors, all this property will revert to the king, because I am a woman and I shall be destitute."

Thus musing one day, knowing that her parents were in the habit of placing an invaluable ruby in their bed, she concealed it when her parents had gone out to wash their heads.

While he was changing his dress, the Brahman thought of the ruby and asked his wife, whether it was still in the bed; she said that she had not seen it when she came away.

Hearing this he ran back quickly.

The daughter after having concealed the ruby, had put water ready for her parents to wash their feet in, and waited.

The Brahman, on arriving, searched all round but not finding (the ruby), said to his daughter: "Darling daughter! have you taken the ruby from out of our bed, after we had gone to wash our heads?"

She said: "I know nothing about it."

When the Brahman heard this, he disputed with his daughter and going to the Judge of the town, to have the case examined, the Judge after examining the daughter and the parents, decided, that it was not (in the bed).

The Brahman, being dissatisfied, went to the Governor, who decided as the Judge has done.

The Brahman being still dissatisfied went to the king, who called the minister and said: "Within seven days you examine into and decide this case, if you do not do so within this time, you shall be ruined;" upon which the minister grew very anxious, and his daughter, seeing this, said, "Oh, my noble father! what are you concerned about?"

"My beloved daughter!" said the minister, "There

are three Brahmans, father, mother, and daughter, and because they cannot find and come to a conclusion about a ruby, the king said, that I should be ruined, therefore I am troubled."

When the daughter heard these words, she said: "Tell the king that I will decide the case within the seven days."

Her father did so, and the king said: "Very well!"

The minister's daughter told her father to call a clever secretary, which he did, and calling the Brahman and his wife she said:

"Oh, you owners of ten millions of property! how is this case?

"Oh, daughter of the great minister!" they said; "from the day we were married, we have treasured up all this property to preserve our children from poverty."

Calling the daughter and asking her, she said: "You are a woman and so am I, when our parents die we shall get no more property than the king gives us."

Having ordered the secretary to write down the exact words, she called the Brahman and his wife and questioned them again.

They said: "Whether the property we have accumulated is little or much, is it not for our children?"

When she heard these words, she ordered the secretary to write them down.

The import of these words was, that undoubtedly the daughter had the ruby.

She told the Brahman and his wife to go and leave Thamodda Seitta Kongmari with her, and that she would have her conducted back after further examining her.

Again summoning the Brahman's daughter and eating and drinking with her, the minister's daughter thought to herself: "The girl has the ruby; by what stratagem can I get possession of it?" and approaching her father, told him, that if he would give her his invaluable ruby, she would be able to get the other ruby, so the minister gave her the ruby, and she nearing the Brahman's daughter, made free with her and they joked together.

Whilst thus making free and joking, she showed the Brahman's daughter the ruby, who, when she saw it said: " Is this your own or somebody's else?"

"It is my father's," she answered, "when my parents die, it will become the king's property, therefore I have concealed it," hearing which, the Brahman's daughter said: "I have one like it."

When the minister's daughter heard these words, she said: "We are both women and of one mind, we also have the same manner of speaking and are both intelligent, we will put our rubies together and conceal them, and let nobody know anything about it."

"It is very like your's my Lady; and as I am afraid my parents may find it, I will put it together with your's," and gave the ruby, taking which, the minister's daughter presented it to her father.

The minister called the secretary and asked him where it had been got from, and the secretary narrated the young lady's management.

The minister said: "Oh, how clever my daughter is;" and went together with the secretary, to present (the ruby) to the king.

On being presented with the ruby, the king asked, whence it had been obtained, and the minister said: my daughter discovered it."

On handing the ruby to the Brahman Oodeitsa, the latter exclaimed: "Oh, Lord, Oh Lord! how did you obtain it?"

" By my power," (45.) answered the king.

The minister's daughter was raised to be queen.

So wise Judges should decide after a searching investigation.

XV. THE CASE OF THE THOO-HTE'S SON, THE ICHNEUMON, THE CAT, AND THE DOG.

In the life time of our Lord Gaunagong (Gonaguna) (46.), the son of a Thoo-hte, and the son of a commoner, were learning the sciences at Tekkatho (Tax-ila) and when each of them was a proficient (as he desired to be), they asked their teacher, what was the good of learning."

The teacher said : " At the begining of the world, there were four great Thoo-hte's in the country of Gahapedee-waitha. (Galapa-ti-vesa) These four Thoo-hte's loved each other very much and did not envy each other their wealth.

Then one of the Thoo-htes died. There was only one son and his mother, the Thoo-hte's wife, called the son and said : " My beloved son, my husband, your father, is dead, and as you are his flesh and blood, you are entitled to the inheritance, but although you are so entitled, you are young yet, therefore go to my husbands relations, the three Thoo-htes, to acquire knowledge," and giving him three hundred pieces of silver, pointed out to him (the three Thoo-htes).

(45.) This is the meaning of the figurative words used by the king: မင်းမျက်စိထည့်၍ i.e. by putting the kings eye into (somebody,) equivalent to conferring the king's power on that person.

(46.) One of the twenty eight Buddhas, who is said to have attained the age of thirty thousand years and the height of thirty cubits. He was perfected under a ရေသဖန်းပင်။ Yay-tha-phan-bing, Ficus lanceolata.

The Thoo-hte's son taking dresses and ornaments, suitable to his rank, went to the three Thoo-htes.

At that instant a man with a dog met with the Thoo-hte's son, who said : "Hollo, man ! will you sell your dog ?"

"If you want to buy him" he replied, "give a hundred pieces of silver for him," so he gave him the price he asked and sent the dog to his mother's house, letting her know all the circumstances.

The Thoo-hte's wife thought, that he had bought (the dog) with the permission of her husband's relations, and fed him well.

One day, on going to a rural feast, (47.) a man came carrying a cat, and the Thoo-hte's son said : "Hollo, man ! will you sell your cat ?"

"If you want to buy her," he replied, "give one hundred pieces of silver for her," so he gave him the price he asked, and sent the cat to his mother in the same manner, (as he had done the dog), and she, thinking, that her son had bought it under the directions of her husband's relations, fed it well.

Another day, when he went to take his food, a man came along, holding an Ichneumon, and the Thoo-hte's son seeing it, said : "Hollo, man ! will you sell your Ichneumon ?"

The man said : "I will."

"Then state your price," said the Thoo-hte's son. "If you want to buy it, give me a hundred pieces of silver for it."

Giving him what he asked, he sent the Ichneumon to

(47.) The word used လယ်ထမင်း။ is ancient Burmese and has become obsolete, all old Burmese works, abound with such ancient words.

his mother also, and she, thinking that it was sent under the instructions of her husband's relations, fed it well.

The Thoo-hte's wife fed the dog and the cat without fear, as they were domestic animals, but the ichneumon being a wild animal, she was afraid of, and did not (continue to) feed it, so the ichneumon grew lean.

The religious teacher of the Thoo-hte's wife, coming to receive his food, (48.) she came down from the house to pour it out, and when he saw her, said: "You, lay-woman, are very thin!" and recited the eight temporal laws. (49.)

"I, (your disciple) (50.) am thin from no other cause," said she, "than because, having let my son go to his father's relations, the three Thoo-hte's to acquire knowledge, after giving him three hundred pieces of silver, he sent me, one day a dog, for which he had given one hundred pieces, on an other day a cat, for which he had given one hundred pieces and on (still) another day an ichneumon, for which he had also given a hundred pieces. Now the dog and and the cat being domestic animals, I am not afraid of, but the incheu-

---

(48.) According to Buddhas teaching, and the monastic rules, the phoongyis or monks in Burmah, are obliged to beg their food, which is call ဆွမ်းခံ။ Htsone-khan.

(49.) The လောကထံတရားရှစ်ပါး။ "eight temporal laws" are, လဒ်သတ်ပကာရှိ သည့် တ ပါး။ မရှိ သည့် လည်း တ ပါး။ Wealth and Poverty; အခြွေအရံရှိသည့်တပါး။မရှိသည့်လည်းတပါး။ Society and Solitude; ကဲ့ရဲ့ခြင်းတပါး။ချီးမွမ်းခြင်းလည်းတပါး။ Reproach and Praise; ချမ်းသာ ခြင်း တ ပါး။ ဆင်းရဲ ခြင်း လည်းတပါး။ Happiness and Misery.

(50.) Laymen never make use of the personal pronoun when speaking to a Phoongyee; they always say: တပည့်တော်။ Tabyeedaw, "Your disciple;" and the Phoongyees address them as တကာ။ Taga, being a contraction of the Pali word ဒါယကာ။ Daraka, i. e: Layman."

mon, being a wild animal, I get frightened at, when I see it therefore, I am lean and hollow-eyed.

The priest told her to set it free in the jangal.

As it is not proper to transgress the words of teachers and parents, and to disobey their orders, she set it free in the jangal, with some food well oiled.

When the ichneumon arrived at the jangal, she considered thus; "The Thoo-hte's son having given a hundred pieces (for me), I came into his possession; he fed me well, and set me free, with my life also, I must repay my banefactor," aud putting the Mani-Zawta (Manijota) (51) ruby, which she got in the jangal, in her mouth, took it to the Thoo-hte's son and said: "This is not an ordinary ruby, but one that will give the wearer of it every thing he wishes for; you will obtain whatever you long for; wear it constantly and do not not let any one else wear it," after saying which, she returned to the jangal.

The Thoo-hte's son longed for a palace, and in the same night, one rose up in front of his house.

All the people, from the King downwards, came to see (the sight), and the King gave the Thoo-hte's son his daughter in marriage.

Soon afterwards, the princess's Brahman teacher came to see if he could discover some particular signs on the Thoo-hte's son; he looked, but saw nothing except the (ruby) ring.

When the Thoo-hte's son had gone out, he entered the palace, and after making flattering speeches to the princess, asked her, whether her husband loved her.

"How can you ask such a question, my Lord Brah-

(51.) "Mani," or, as some write it: "Muni," is (Pali) "Gem," and "jota" is (Pali) "precious."

man?" replied she, "he is only a Thoo-hte's son, whilst I am a princess."

"If he love you so much, you have perhaps been allowed to wear his ring?" insinuated the Brahman.

"If I have not worn it," returned she, "pray who has?"

One day the princess asked the Thoo-hte's son to let her wear his ring, and he, loving her extremely, took it off and gave it to her, charging her, not to take it off to show it to any one, but to wear it constantly on her finger.

One day, when the Thoo-hte's son was absent, the Brahman came again, and addressed her with his smooth phrases; she said: "I am wearing the ring you spoke of the other day."

"Are you," he asked, "where is it?"

"Here," she replied, displaying it.

"Take it off and show it to me, my daughter," he begged, and at last on her nurse saying: "Dear young lady! the teacher begs for it so earnestly, please let him see it!" she took it off and gave it to him.

The instant, the Brahman received it, he assumed the appearance of a crow and flew away to the middle of the ocean, whither no one could follow him, and there dwelt in a palace.

When the Thoo-hte's son returned, and heard that the Brahman had taken the ring, he said to the princess: "Although I particularly charged you, not to show the ring, you did so, and the result is, that it is now in the middle of the ocean, from whence it cannot be recovered."

After speaking these words he remained brooding (over his loss).

One day a party of Fairies came to bathe in a tank covered with water-lilies, not far from where the Thoo-hte's son dwelt, and having taken off their neck-laces, they laid them down on the bank; where the cat, brought up by the Thoo-hte's son, found them.

The fairies came to the cat and begged her to return their necklaces saying that they were only fit for Nats and notfor mortals.

The cat said: "If I do it, you must make a road for me to travel to the place where the Brahman is living in his palace in the middle of the ocean; on this condition only will I return then."

The fairies made the road and the cat crept stealthily along it until she arrived at the palace, where she found the Brahman asleep, with the ring on his finger, she then slipped the ring off and quietly brought it back and delivered it to her master, in return for his kindness, saying: "You have paid a great price for me, and have fed and taken care of me ever since."

As for the Brahman, he fell into the sea and was drowned, whilst the Thoo-hte's son, having recovered the ring, had every wish that he formed fulfilled.

After a time, a Band of five hundred Robbers came to kill the Thoo-hte's son and take away his ring, when the dog thought to himself; "They have come to kill my master, who has purchased me for so high a price and has treated me so well," so he flew at the leader of the band and bit him to death, and threw his body down a well. Seeing this, the rest of the robbers fled in dismay.

The next morning the dog said to his master "I had no sleep last night; I had hard work too;" and on being asked to explain, he related as follows: "Five hundred robbers came last night, to kill you and take away your ring so I killed their chief and threw him into the well and the rest fled. In return for the many favors you have confered upon me, I have watched over your life and property."

"Ah," replied the Thoo-hte's son, "Every one blamed

me for giving a hundred pieces for you, who are but an animal, but I owe all my prosperity to three animals, each of which I purchased at that price."

Thus saying he went into the jangal and brought back the ichneumon to live with the others.

The ichneumon claimed precedence at their meals; the dog said that he had the right of precedence; and the cat said, that she was entitled to it.

The ichneumen said: "I am the one who first gave the ring."

The cat said to the Ichneumon: "After the gift which you had made, became the property of the Brahman, I took the neck-laces of the Fairies, and by means of the road, they made for me, recovered the ring; have not I therefore given the wealth (to our master)?"

The dog said: "When the five hundred robbers came to kill the Thoo-hte's son and take your wealth, I killed their chief and cast him into the well, whereupon the rest of the band fled, and thus I am the preserver of our master's life as well as of his wealth; I have saved him from destruction, therefore I am entitled to precedence."

At that time there was in the Kambauza (Kamboja) country, in the Kingdom of Maderit (Madaraja), a princess, the daughter of King Dammarit named Thoodamma Tsāri, (Sudammachári), who had a perfect knowledge of the ten laws (52), was deeply versed in the civil and criminal codes,

---

(52.) The ten laws here referred to, are no doubt the ပါရမီဆယ်ပါး။ the ten Primary virtues, viz: ဒါန။ Dana—Alms-giving. သီလ။ (Sila) Theela—performance of religious duties .နိက္ခမ။ Neikkhama—Secluded ife; ပညာ (Panya) Peenya—Wisdom, Prudence. ဝီရိယ (Viriya) Weereeya—Diligence. ခန္တီ Khanti—Patience. သစ္စာ (Sachcha) Thitsa—Veracity. အဓိဋ္ဌာန်။

who lived in a separate palace, (53) and whose fame had spread to the eight quarters of the world, so that the illustrious of every nation came to her for judgment.

The ichneumon, the dog and the cat, disputing, agreed to go to, and abide by the decision of the princess.

The ichneumon said: "The Thoo-hte's son gave as much as a hundred pieces (of silver) for me, fed and tended me well, and gave me my liberty. Bearing this in mind, and because he was my benefactor, I gave him the Mani-Zawta (Mani jota) ruby ring, by means of which he obtained a palace, which spruug up (out of the ground); Therefore I am entitled to have precedence."

Then the cat said: "The property given by the ichneumon, was taken by the Brahman, I recovered it; Thus the Thoo-hte's son enjoyed his fortune, therefore I am entitled to precedence.

After this the Dog said: "The property given by the ichneumon, was lost after its receipt, and the cat recovered it, after which robbers came to steal it; I bit and killed the chief, upon which the robbers ran away. I have saved the Thoo-hte's son's wealth as well as his life, therefore I am entitled to precedence."

Adi-htana—Constancy. မေတ္တာ။ Mietta—Benevolence; and ဥပေက္ခာ Oopekha—Impartiality.

(53.) A princess who is greatly beloved by the King, and whom he does not want to marry; or a princess who of her own accord wishes to remain single and who devotes herself to the observance of the religious duties and the ten virtues, has a separate palace built for her sole use, this palace, the roof of which is crowned by one steeple only, instead of five, or seven, or nine as the King's and other members of the royal family, is called a တပင်တိုင်ပြာသာဒ်။ Tabing-taing-pyathat.

When they had ended, princess Thoodamma Tsāri thus pronounced her Judgment: " The dog in addition, to saving his master's treasures, prolonged his life also, therefore he is entitled to the first place in preference to you; but, verily! among animals there are none, that so well understood to repay a debt of gratitude."

Thus ends the story of the Dog, the Cat, and the Ichneumon, from which you may learn, that although man is superior to amimals, yet, kinduess to them will be rewarded.

XVI. THE CASE OF THE THOO-HTE'S DAUGHTER AND HER THREE LOVERS.

At the time (of the preceding story) there lived in Kambauza (Kamboja) four rich men, and these four rich men loved each other very much.

Three Thoo-htes had each one son, whilst the fourth had an only daughter, a perfect beauty, and to her all three young men sent a messenger.

The first one (through his messenger) promised that he would, if she should die before she was fifteen, perform her funeral rites with every care.

The second sent to say, that, if she should die before her fifteenth year, he would collect her remains.

The third sent to say, that, if she should die before her fifteenth year he would watch at her tomb.

To each of these offers the parents answered: " It is well!"

The maiden died before she had attained her fifteenth year, and the parents desired the young men to perform their respective promises.

The first in accordance with his engagement performed the rites of cremation; the second according to his promise, collected and brought her bones (to the tomb); and the third kept watch, as he had engaged to do, over them in the cemetery.

At this time a hermit—Jogee, who came from the Himalayan forests saw the watch-man and asked: "Young man what are you watching for?"

"I am watching over the bones (of the dead) my Lord!" replied he.

"Would you wish (the dead) restored to life?"

"I would," replied the youth, upon which (she) became a beautiful maiden as before. (54.)

Then the first of the three Thoo-hte's sons said: "I carried her corpse to the funeral pile and burnt it, ought she not therefore to be mine?"

The second said:" I collected her bones, ought she not to be mine?"

The third said: "Whilst I was watching in the cemetery, she returned to life; ought she not to be mine?"

"What is the good of us three disputing with each other? Let us submit to the decision of the princess Thoodamma-tsari" they said.

So they all three went to the princess and when they had related all the circumstances to her, she said: "I understand this matter; one of you burnt the corpse of the maiden, and went his way; the other collected her bones, and went his way; but the third kept watch in the cemetery, although the family of a cemetery watchman is degraded to

---

(54.) Hermits are supposed to obtain, through their spiritual life, supernatural powers. Some of the most gifted hermits are celebrated in the Indian national epos, the "Mahabharata," see the songs: "Narada's predictions," Sakuntala," etc.

the seventh generation, (55) and it was during his watch that the maiden returned to life; therefore: "as he kept her company in death, he is entitled to be her partner in life!" was the decision of the princess Thoodamma-tsari.

XVII. THE CASE OF THE THOO-HTE'S SON AND HIS THREE WIVES.

At the same time (of the preceding story) the son of a Thoo-hte of no particular note, who was married when he was ten years old, used constantly to say: "If I should ever die from the bite of a snake, do not bury my corpse by cremation, but fasten it upon a raft, and set it adrift."

One day this man *was* bitten by a snake and he died, so in obedience to his oft repeated instructions, his wife and his relatives bound his body upon a raft and set it adrift.

Driftiug down the river it came to a large town, in which lived a snake charmer, whose three daughters had just then come down to wash their heads. Seeing the raft, the eldest of them cried out; "It is a raft with the body of a man upon it.!"

The second said: "Who knows, whether his death has not been caused by the bite of a snake?" and swimming (56) to the raft, brought it to the shore, while the youngest ran to call her father. Their father came and by applying medicines and charms, restored (the young man) to life.

(55.) Up to the present the grave-diggers or chandalas who are also watchmen of the grave-yards, are, contrary to the spirit of Buddhism, looked upon as a degraded caste.

(56.) Most of the towns and villages in Burmah being situated on the banks of rivers, or creeks, there are very few Burmans, male or female who cannot swim.

Then the eldest daughter said: "I saw him first, he ought to be my husband."

The second said: "I swam and brought the raft to the shore, he ought to be mine."

The youngest said: I called our father who applying medicines and charms, brought him to life again, therefore he ought to be my husband."

Then the eldest said; "It is not becoming in us three sisters, to be quarreling about the possession of the same man; let us be prudent and restrain ourselves, my sisters, and let this man go."

"It is true what you say, sister" they said, and they tied a magic thread (57) round (the young man's) neck, whereupon he was transformed into a small parrot and flew away.

The little parrot flew back to his own country, where he settled in the King's garden, living upon the fruit there.

When the gardener delivered the fruit and the flowers to the King, the latter said: "Hallo, gardener! formerly the fruit and flowers used to look well, but now they do not."

"Ah, your Majesty!" replied the gardener, "formerly

(57.) The belief in witchcraft and in the magic virtue of certain mixtures, muntras and charms, is as unshaken now, as it was a thousand years ago, among both Burmans and Talaings, and they have numerous appellations for them, such as: မျက်နှာပွင့်။ Myet-nha-pwing, i. e. a medicine to excite love; အနုဆေး။ Anoo-hsai, the same; မန်းရေ။ Man-yai and ချည်မန်း။ Khyee-man, i. e. Water and Thread into which the desired virtue is infused, by repeating a muntra over it; ပရိတ်ချည် Pareik-khyee and ပရိတ်ရေ water and thread, used as a preservative from evil, etc, there were no parrots, but now there is a small one, which I cannot drive away."

"If that is the case," said the King "let all the bird-catchers set traps for him."

So they set traps and caught him, but as they had pity on him, they did not kill him, but presented him to the King, who, on account of his beauty, gave him to his daughter.

The princess, continually playing with the parrot, saw the thread, and taking it off, he instantly became a handsome young man; fastening the thread on him again, he was changed back into a parrot.

Now from taking off the thread at night and fastening it on again in the day, after some time had elapsed, the princess' figure lost its symetry, which coming to the king's ear, he sent for the Chief Justice and had the matter investigated (58).

Owing to the examining and searching that ensued, the little parrot got frightened and flew out of the window, when the thread caught in the window frame and broke off, so becoming a handsome young man again, he ran up into the house of a Thoo-hte's, who was eating his rice with his wife and daughter and questioned the young man, who related what had happened to him. He was thereupon allowed to dip his hand into the dish and to eat with them.

The servants of the Chief Justice, thinking that a thief had gone into the Thoo-hte's house, arrived in pursuit, when the Thoo-hte's wife said:

"We are taking our meals with our daughter and son-in-law, but as you say there is a thief, try and catch him," and consented to a search being made, but the servants of the Chief-Justice not finding any one, went away.

(58.) There is nothing immoral in the princess' behaviour; vide Note 27, para; 3. She had the

The Thoo-hte, seeing that the young man was very handsome, married him to his daughter.

Now the princess in consequence of her separation from the young man fell ill and the king said to her: "Darling daughter, what is the reason of your illness?"

She revealed to him all, and that the separation from the young man was the cause of her illness; whereupon he ordered that search should be made for him.

Then preparing a great entertainment, he sent for the rich, the wealthy, the nobles and the judges to come and witness it.

They all came accordingly, and the young man also came with the Thoo-hte's daughter.

The princess on seeing him, cried, out; "This is my husband!"

At the same time, she who had been the young man's wife before his death, saw him also and exclaimed: "Oh, my husband! We set him adrift, bound to a raft, when he died of a snake-bite, but if he has not really died, I claim him as my husband."

The princess said: "It was only from fear of my father, that he ran away."

The Thoo-hte's daughter said: "When the servants of the Chief Justice would have killed this young man, thinking him to be a thief, my parents by their prudence, saved him and gave him to me in marriage; ought he not then to be mine?"

Thus they disputed and the king said: "I will not makes use of compulsion, but go and submit to the decision of the princess Thoodamma tsāri." Accordingly they went

---

choice of a husband and was only afraid the King might not approve of her choice; the sequal shows, that the young man was looked upon as her husband.

to her and the princess enquired of them the circumstances of the case.

She who had been the young man's wife before his death, stated as follows; "As my husband died of a snake bite, his body, in accordance with his wishes, was not burnt, but set adrift, fastened on a raft; if he has not died after all, ought he not to be my husband?"

The princess said: "This young man having been transformed into a parrot, destroyed our fruit and flowers, wherefore the bird-catchers were called and ordered to entrap him; they did so and got him, upon which he was brougt to me. After he had become my husband, my father caused enquiries to be made upon which the young man fled, ought he not therefore to be my husband?"

The Thoo-hte's daughter said: "When the king's servants pursued the young man, thinking him to be a thief, he, fearing for his life, took refuge in our house, my father managed so as to save his life, and gave him to me in marriage; ought he not therefore to be my husband?"

Princess Thoodamma-tsāri then gave Judgment as follows: "As the young man's first wife buried her husband on the water, he cannot now be her husband, even though he is alive again. With regard to the princess, If on the king's sending the Chief-Justice he had succeeded in arresting the young man, she could not have prevented his death, and as he would have been lost to her then, she cannot claim him as her husband now. The parents of his present wife prevented the death of him, who was (as good as) dead, therefore let her be his partner in life.

VOCABULARY.

VOCABULARY

အ။

အကုဋေ၊ (Pali) ten millions.

အကောင်၊ a dead body, a corpse,

အကျင့်၊ a habit, a deed.

အကျိုး၊ a consequence, a good result, benefit.

အကြင်သူ၊ whoso, whoever, that man.

အကြားအမြင်၊ from အ၊ substantive prefix, ကြား၊ to hear, မြင်၊ to see; e. g. hearing and seeing.

အကြိမ်၊ a time, a turn.

——ကြိမ်၊——များစွာ၊ many times.

အကြောင်း၊ a consequence, a circumstance, business, cause.

——မျိုး၊ all the circumstances; everything concerning.

အကျွမ်းဝင်၊ to be well acquainted, familiar with; to familiarize.

အချင်းချင်း၊ one another, among each other, mutually

အနှိ၊ a nurse, an attendant on children.

အခြင်းအရာ၊ same as အကြောင်း။

အခွင့်၊ permission; privilege; opportunity; business.

အငုံ၊ a flower bud.

အငြင်းအခုံ၊ from အ၊ substantive prefix and ငြင်းခုံ to dispute; contradict; deny e. g. a dispute.

အစ၊ beginning with; from—to.

အစိုးရ to have authority over; Government; Government Officers.

အဆုံးအဖြတ်၊ (from ဆုံးဖြတ်၊ to decide) a decision.

အဆောင်အရောင်၊ articles of use or ornament, indicative of rank.

အဆွေခင်ပွန်း a relative, a friend.

———အမျိုး၊ a relative, a kinsman.

အညီအမျှ၊ in equal parts.

အညှာ၊ the stalk of a leaf; the stem of a flower or fruit.

အတတ်၊ science; skill.

အထိမ်း၊ အထိန်း၊ a nurse; a keeper.

အဓိပ္ပာယ်၊ (Pali,) meaning, import, explanation.

အနဃ၊ အနန္တ၊ အနန္တ၊ (Pali) immeasurable; invaluable.

အန္တရာယ်၊ (Pali) danger, evil, calamity.

အနှိုင်၊ အနိုင့်၊ force, constraint.

အပါယ်၊ (Pali) a state of punishment.

အပါး၊ the space near, (a thing or person.)

အပေါင်းအရု၊ from အ၊ the substantive prefix, and ပေါင်း၊ unite; ရု၊ collect, gather; e. g. a lump; a heap.

———အဖက်၊———အဖော်၊ companion, associate.

အပြစ်၊ an evil result, punishment,—opposed to အကျိုး၊

———ကင်း၊ to be free from punishment.

———ရှိ၊ to be subject to, to deserve punishment.

အပွင့်၊ a flower; blossom.

အဖိုအရ၊ a part; a share.

အဘယ်၊ what, how, where?

အဖြစ်၊ a state of being; condition.

အမတ်၊ a nobleman.

အမေးအမြန်း၊ an enquiry.

အမောင်၊ brother.

အမြီး၊ a tail.

အမွေ၊ an inheritance.

———ခံ၊ to inherit ; an heir.

အမြွက်စကား၊ a suggestion ; a hint.

အမှုသည်၊ a party to a law-suit.

အမျှဝေ၊ to divide and distribute equally.

အရင်းအနှီး stock in trade, a capital to trade with.

အရပ်၊ a place ; a country.

———လေးမျက်နှာ၊ from အရပ်၊ as above ; လေး four, and မျက်နှာ a quarter of the heavens ; a cardinal point ; e. g. from the places of all four quarters, fig : every where.

အရံခြံ၊ အခြံအရံ၊ attendants ; people in waiting.

အရာ၊ business—affair.

အရိပ်၊ shade, a hint.

အရောင်အဆင်၊ appearance.

———ဆောင်၊ to assume appearance.

အရိုးအဖတ်၊ from အရိုး၊ bone ; and အဖတ်၊ that what remains of a thing, after its useful parts or portions have been made use of ; e. g. refuse ; rubbish.

အရွယ်၊ age.

အရှက်၊ shame.

———ကွဲ၊ to be put to shame.

အရှင်၊ lord ; master ; an owner.

———မ၊ from အရှင်၊ as above ; and မ၊ female ; e. g. mistress, lady.

အလမ္ပာယ်၊ a snake catcher ; a snake trainer.

အလိမ္မာ၊ cleverness.

အဝဓာန်း၊ (Pali) precaution ; circumspection, consideration ; အဝဓာန်။

အသာ၊ gentle.

အသရေ၊ reputation ; character.

အသွင်၊ form.

———ပြု၊ to assume (the) form ; to personate.

အသွေးအရည်၊ offspring.

အံ့ဘွယ်၊ အံ့ဖွယ်၊ အံ့ဖွယ်သရဲ၊ wonderful; a wonderful thing.

အာစာရ၊ (Pali), habit; custom; a deed, same as အကျင့်။

အာဏာ၊ (Pali), authority ; an order.

အာရုံ၊ an object of thought or sense.

———ပြု၊ to dwell upon in mind ; to make an object of thought or desire.

အားမခံ၊ အာမခံ၊ (Pali) to agree to, to stand security for.

အိပ်၊ to lie down.

———ပျော်၊ to sleep, to be asleep.

အိမ်တော်၊ from အိမ်၊ a house ; and တော်၊ an honorfic affix in compliment to persons of high rank, the king and a deity, any thing belonging to them; e. g. a palace.

အောင်းမေ့၊ to remember ; bear in mind ; to think.

အိုးထိမ်းသည်၊အိုးထိန်းသည်၊ a potter.

ဥပမာ၊ (Pali) a representation ; a comparison ; similitude.

ဥပါယ်၊ (Pali) a means, devise, an artifice.

———တမည်၊ တမျည်၊ same.

ဥယည် or ဥယျည်၊ an orchard ; a garden.

က။

ကင်း၊ to be free from, separate from.

ကန်စင်းရိုး၊ a ridge of earth in rice fields.

ကမ္ဘာ၊ the world.

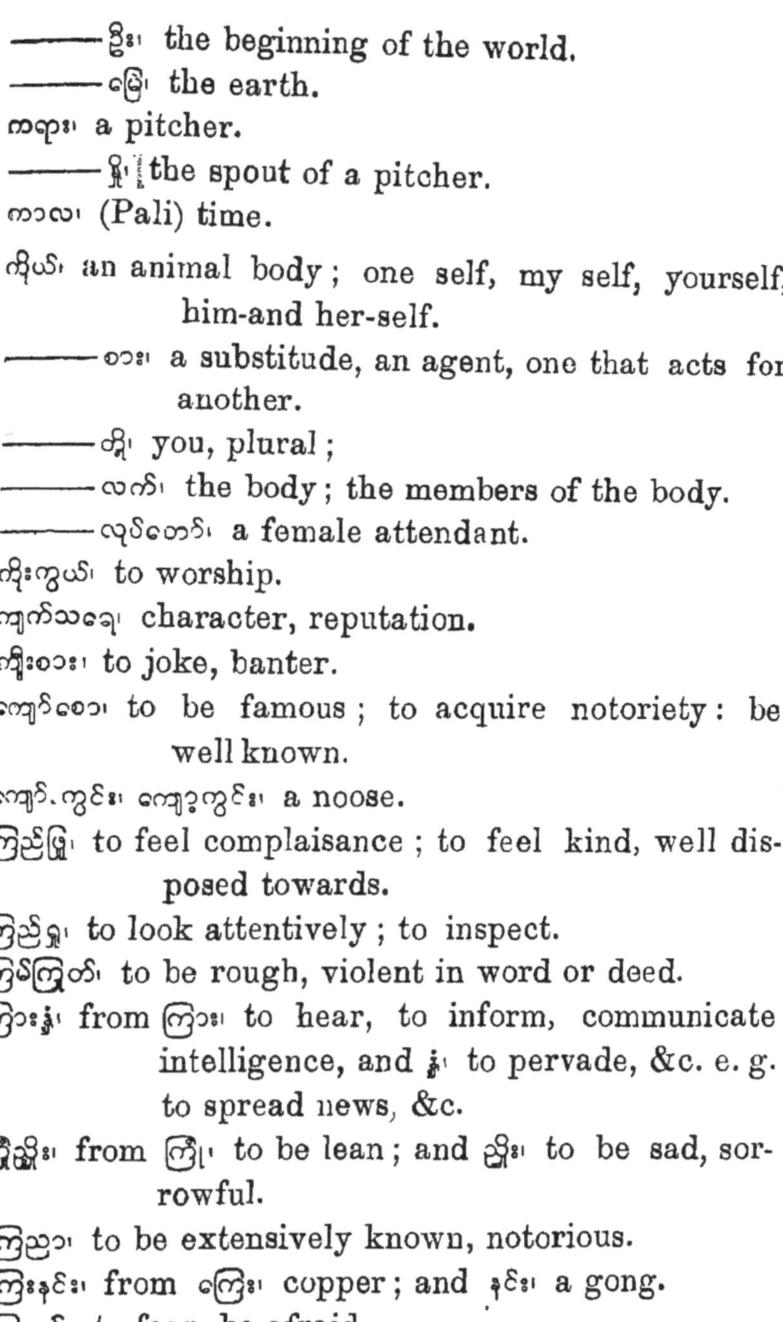

———ဦး၊ the beginning of the world.

———မြေ၊ the earth.

ကရား၊ a pitcher.

———နှ၊ the spout of a pitcher.

ကာလ၊ (Pali) time.

ကိုယ်၊ an animal body; one self, my self, yourself, him-and her-self.

———စား၊ a substitude, an agent, one that acts for another.

———တို့၊ you, plural;

———လက်၊ the body; the members of the body.

———လုပ်တော်၊ a female attendant.

ကိုးကွယ်၊ to worship.

ကျက်သရေ၊ character, reputation.

ကျီးစား၊ to joke, banter.

ကျော်စော၊ to be famous; to acquire notoriety: be well known.

ကျော့ကွင်း၊ ကျော့ကွင်း၊ a noose.

ကြည်ဖြူ၊ to feel complaisance; to feel kind, well disposed towards.

ကြည့်ရှု၊ to look attentively; to inspect.

ကြမ်းကြုတ်၊ to be rough, violent in word or deed.

ကြားနှံ့၊ from ကြား၊ to hear, to inform, communicate intelligence, and နှံ့၊ to pervade, &c. e. g. to spread news, &c.

ကြုံညှိုး၊ from ကြုံ၊ to be lean; and ညှိုး၊ to be sad, sorrowful.

ကြေညာ၊ to be extensively known, notorious.

ကြေးနင်း၊ from ကြေး၊ copper; and နင်း၊ a gong.

ကြောက်၊ to fear, be afraid.

——— ခွန် or ခွံ၊ same.

ကြောင်ကြ၊ to be concerned, anxious, troubled about.

ကြိုက်၊ to like, love.

ကွယ်ပျောက်၊ to disappear, die.

ကျွန်၊ a slave, a servant:

———တော်၊ from above, and တော်၊ a honorific affix in compliment to persons of high rank, the king and a deity; and things belong- to them; e. g. a king's subject, or slave; *pron.* I, masculine—used in addressing a superior.

———မ၊ and ကျွန်တော်မ၊ feme. I, fiminine.

ကြွယ်၊ to be oppulent, wealthy.

ကြွေ၊ to fall off, as leaves or fruit.

ခ॥

ခက်ထန်၊ to be hard to deal with, severe, rigorous.

ခင်ပွန်း၊ a spouse; a correlate in marriage, whether husband or wife; in composition with အဆွေ၊ and မိတ်၊ a friend.

ခစား၊ to attend on, wait upon.

ခဏ၊ (Pali) an instant, a moment.

ခပ်သိမ်း၊ all, the whole.

ခမည်းတော်၊ a father, (honorific).

ခရီ၊ a journey; a voyage; the distance between two places.

———သည်၊ and—သွား၊ a traveller.

ခဝါသည်၊ a washerman.

ခါးဆစ်၊ the joint of the small of the back.

ခေါင်း၊ the head.

———လျှော်၊ to wash the head. N. B. လျှော် is pronounced: shaw.

ခိုက်၊ during, whilst.

ခိုးသူ၊ from ခိုး၊ to steal and သူ၊ a person; e. g. a thief သူခိုး။

ချည်း၊ only, nothing, but.

ချီးမွမ်း၊ to praise, applaud.

ချော်၊ to slip; err; to make a mistake.

ခြေရင်တော်၊ from ခြေရင်း၊ the place for the feet, and တော် honorific affix, also ခြေတော်ရင်း။

ခြုံ၊ a cluster of bushes; a jangal; a thicket.

ဂ။

ဂင်္ဂါ၊ the Ganges.

ဂန္တရာ၊ (Pali)—ခရီး a resting or halting place on a journey.

ဂျီ၊ the barking deer.

င။

င၊ ငါ၊ *pron.* I, and in certain constructions: my, me; indicative of superiority in the speaker.

င၊ abbr: of ငါး၊ a fish.

———ကျင်း၊ a gudgeon.

ငဆ၊ a term of reproach, like နင်၊ you, thou.

ငိုမည်တမ်း၊ to cry loud.

ငြင်း၊ to contradict; to refuse to; to object to.

ငှက်ခတ်သွား၊ bird catchers.

စ။

စက္ခု၊ (Pali) the eye.

———ဝိညာဏ်၊ or ဝိညာဉ်၊ from စက္ခု၊ the eye and ဝိညာဉ်၊ the soul; e. g. sight.

စင်ကြယ်၊ pure; clear.

စည်းစိမ်၊ wealth ; the enjoyment of any comfort, wealth, &c.

စဉ်းလဲ၊ to use artifice (in a bad sense); to cheat.

စံစား၊ to enjoy.

စာချီး၊ a secretary.

စိတ်၊ (Pali စိတ္တ၊) the mind ; temper.

———ကောက်၊ to be put out of temper, to be irritable ; ill tempered.

———ချုပ်၊ to restrain ones temper.

စေတမန်၊ a messenger ; an ambassador.

ရူးစမ်း၊ to try.

စေ့စပ်၊ to join by a union of parts.

စိုင်၊ a wild ox.

စိုးရိမ်၊ to be concerned, anxious, troubled about.

ဆ။

ဆက်၊ to offer respectfully ; to present as to a king or governor.

ဆင်ချေ၊ (better ဆင်ခြေ) a plea ; an argument.

ဆင်ခြင်၊ to consider, reflect on.

ဆတ်၊ a large species of deer ; an elk.

ဆည်းပူး၊ to collect, treasure up, accumulate.

ဆတ္တာ၊ ဆတ္တာသည်၊ a barber.

ဆယ်၊ to take up or out of the water, to extricate, to save.

ဆီးတား၊ to impede ; obstruct ; prevent.

ဆုလဒ်၊ a reward ; a present.

ဆေးဝါး၊ a medicine, a drug.

ဆောင်နှင်း၊ to give in marriage (honorific).

ဆွမ်း၊ cooked rice for priests.

———ခံ to receive such rice.

ဆွေမျိုးသားချင်း၊ relatives.

ဇ။

ဇန်၊ or ဈာန်၊ a state of mind.

ဇောတ၊ a precious stone.

ဈ။

ဈောဂီ၊ a jogee or fakir.

ည။

ည၊ night.

ညဦး၊ the evening.

ညီအစ်မ၊ from ညီမ၊ a woman's younger sister, and အစ်မ၊ a woman's elder sister; e. g. sisters.

ညီမျှ၊ to be equal ; in equal parts.

ညောင်ပင်၊ the banian tree.

ညောင်ရေ၊ any holy water; the water from an urn or vase in which flowers are placed, as a religious offering.

ညှိုးငယ်၊ ညှိုငယ်၊ to be sad in mind, or countenance.

ညွှန်ပြ၊ to show, point out.

တ။

တကယ်၊ indeed, certainly.

———ပင်၊ same, really, if indeed.

တကာမ၊ (from the Pali ဒါယကာမ၊) a lay woman.

တငါး၊ a fisherman.

တတ်မက်၊ ထင်မက်၊ to have a desire for, to covet.

တန်ခိုး၊ (from တန်ခိုး၊) power.

တပ်ချ၊ to encamp.

တပ်စွန်၊ to feel strong passion for.

တပည့်၊ a scholar, a disciple (wrongly spelled တပြည့် in the M. S.)

တပည့်တော်၊ *pron*. I, masculine, used in addressing religious teachers.

———မ၊ (a female disciple ;) *pronoun* I, feminine.

တပန်၊ again ; once more.

တမည်၊ တမျည်၊ see ဥပါယ်၊

တမန်၊ see စေတမန်၊

တရား၊ law ; moral principle ; right ; equity ; justice.

———နာ၊ to hear preaching.

တံစိုး၊———လက်ဆောင်၊ a present ; a bribe.

တိရိစ္ဆာန်၊ (Pali,) an animal.

တောအုပ်၊ a thick forest.

တောင့်တ၊ to long for.

တောင်းပန်း၊ to beg pardon ; to intreat.

တိုက်တွန်း၊ to instigate.

ထ။

ထင်ရှား၊ to be conspicuous, well known.

ထိန်းမြား၊ ထိမ်းမြား၊ to marry, unite in marriage ; (polite.)

ထေရ်၊ (pronounce ထည်း) (Pali) မထေရ်၊ abbr. of မဟာ great and ထေရာ၊ a priest ; a buddhist monk or priest of reputed sanctity.

ထောပနာ၊ ထောမနာ၊ (Pali) to laud, praise.

ထွန်းပ၊ to shine ; to be distinguished, conspicuous, to emit light.

ဒ။

ဒါယကာ၊ (Pali) a layman, abbr. to တကာ၊

———မ၊ (Pali) a lay woman, abbr. to တကာမ.

ဒီပ၊ (Pali) an island.

ဒုရင်ခမောင်း၊ a canopy.

ဒေါသ၊ (Pali) anger, passion.

ဓ။

ဓမ္မသတ်၊ (Pali) a code of law ; a Civil Code.

ဓါတ်၊ (Pali ဓါတု၊) an element; the constituent part of anything.

န॥

နက်နဲ၊ to be intellectually deep, profound.

နဂါး၊ a dragon.

နည်း၊ a rule, a precedent; manner, custom.

——— to be few, not many.

နန်းပြာသာဒ်၊ a royal palace.

နံ့၊ spirit, as opposed to ရုပ်၊ matter.

နိဂဏ္ဍိ၊ (Pali) contraction of နိဂဏ္ဍဗိဏ္ဍိ၊? the doctrine of abjuration.

နှစ်သက်၊ to like, to be pleased with, to love.

နှံ့၊ to pervade, to be diffused through or over all the parts.

နှိုးဆော်၊ to excite, to rouse.

ပ॥

ပဉ္စ၊ (Pali) five.

ပညာ၊ (Pali) wisdom; prudence.

ပဋိညာဏ်၊ (Pali) ပဋိဉာဉ်၊ assent, agreement.

ပဒ္မမြား၊ a ruby.

ပတ်လုံး၊ applied to words of time; whole circuit or duration; e. g. တနှစ်ပတ်လုံး၊ during the whole year. တသက်ပတ်လုံး၊ during the whole life.

ပန်ကြား၊ to ask leave, to beg, petition.

ပရဝဏ်၊ a fence forming the enclosure of a sacred place.

ပီတိ၊ (Pali) joy; pleasure.

ဗိဇ္ဇောဆေး၊ ဘိသဇ္ဇောဆေး၊ (Pali) curative medicine, as distinguished from ဓါတ်ဆေး၊ dietary medicine.

ပုခက်၊ (from ပခက်၊) a swinging cradle.

ပုဏ္ဏား၊ (Pali) a brahman.

ပုထုဇန်၊ ပုထုဇဉ်၊ one who is only entering the road to perfection.

ပုန်းရှောင်၊ to conceal one self, hide.

ပုံ၊ shape, form ; a figure, comparison.

———ပြ၊ to show by figure, to represent.

ပူဇော်၊ to make an offering in token of homage or worship.

ပူပန်၊ to be troubled, distressed.

ပေးစား၊ to give in marriage—(common.)

ပေါင်းအိုး၊ ———ချောင်၊ } a pot or vessel with perforated bottom.

ပေါင်းဖော်၊ to associate with ; to keep company.

ပြစ်မှား၊ to transgress, to sin against.

ပြည့်စုံ၊ to be possessed of, replete with ; accomplished.

ပြာသာဒ်၊ a graduated turret, surmounting the roof of a palace, royal boat, and monasteries—hence, also a palace.

ပြဿနာ၊ a question that forms a subject for discussion.

ပြုကျင့်၊ to do, perform.

ပြောင်းပြန်၊ one thing for the other, one end for the other, contrarily, up side down.

ဖ။

ဖန်ဆင်း၊ to make, create.

ဖီတား၊ to prevent, hinder.

ဖုတ်၊ to roast or burn, by putting on or into the fire.

ဖုံးလွှမ်း၊ to cover, overspread.

ဖေါက်ပြန်၊ to break a promise, to apostatize.

ဖေါင်၊ a raft; a yacht; a handsome boat for travelling.

ဖြည်းညှင်း၊ to be slow, gentle.

ဘ။

ဘရက်၊ဘယက်၊ ornaments for the neck; a necklace.

———တန်ဆာ၊ (pronounced တဇာ၊)—same.

ဘာသာ၊ (Pali) language, custom.

ဘုန်း၊ glory, fame, power.

ဘေး၊ danger, calamity.

မ။

မက်မော၊ to covet, to long for.

မကောင်းမှု၊ demerit.

မင်းအိမ်၊ from မင်း၊ a ruler, a governor; and အိမ်၊ a house; hence a palace.

မည်ဆန်၊ not common, uncommon, extraordinary.

မဏိ၊ (Pali) a gem brilliant, precious, but the idea of the former predominating.

မတ္တမရှု၊ from မ၊ negative prefix, and တ္တရှု၊ straight, e. g. not straight.

မထိမဲ့မြင်၊ irreverently, disrespectfully.

မန္တရာ၊ a charm or spell.

မနော၊ (Pali) the mind.

မဟာထေရ်၊ see ထေရ်၊

မာန် (Pali မာန) pride, anger.

———ကြီး၊ to be in a great passion.

မိဖုရား၊ မိဘုရား၊ a queen.

မုတ်ဆိုး၊ မုဆိုး၊ a huntsman.

မောင်း၊ a burmese gong.

———ကြေးနှင်း၊ same.

မောဟ၊ (Pali) folly, ignorance.

မိုးကြိုး၊ a thunderbolt.

မိုးသောက်၊ the dawn of day.

မျက်မုန်းကြိုး၊ to resent, hate, feel ill will.

မျက်မှောက်၊ in presence.

မျက်ရည်၊ a tear.

မြင့်မိုရ်၊ from မြင့်၊ high; and မိုရ်၊ the Meru mountain; e. g, the high Meru.

မြတ်နိုး၊ to love, like, (honorific.)

မြုတာ၊———အိုး၊ a pot with a long neck and an open mouth.

မြောက်၊ to be raised, elevated; above.

မြို့ကွန်၊ the governor of a city, (now obsolete.)

မွန်ရည်၊ to be elegant; excellent; good.

မြွေ၊ a snake, serpent.

———ပါ၊ an ichneumon.

မှိုင်၊ to be lost in thought, to be downcast.

မျှော၊ to set afloat.

မျှော်၊ to expect, wait for.

မြှောက်၊ to raise, elevate.

ယ။

ယမန်၊ recently, lately.

ယာ၊ a cultivated piece of ground.

———ရှင်၊ the owner of such.

ယုတ်၊—မာ၊ to be mean, vile, wicked.

ယုံ၊ to believe, trust in.

ယောက္ခမ၊ a father-in-law, or mother-in-law.

ရ။

ရက်ရက်စက်စက်၊ to be very cruel, unfeeling.

ရည်၊ to aim at, have reference to.

ရန်၊ quarrel, enmity.

———ဖြစ်၊ to quarrel.

———သူ၊ an enemy.

ရသေ့၊ an ascetic, a hermit.

ရဟန္တာ one who has gained perfection. an Ariya အရိယာ။

ရဟန်း၊ see ထေရ်၊

ရာဇသတ်၊ a criminal law, code.

ရာန်သူ၊ see ရန်သူ၊

ရုပ်၊ matter, as opposed to နာ်၊ spirit.

ရေကန်၊ an artificial pond, tank.

ရောဂ၊ ရောဂါ၊ (Pali) disease.

ရိုသေ၊ to respect, reverence.

ရှာဖွေ၊ to seek, search for.

ရှုံး၊ to fail, to lose.

လ။

လက်ဆောင်၊ a present.

လက်သား၊ an underling, assistant.

လက္ခဏာ၊ (Pali) a sign, characteristic.

လင်္ကာသုတ္တ၊ from လင်္ကာ၊ poetry; and သုတ္တ၊ (Pali) a rule e. g. rules of poetry, hence poetry.

လည်းကောင်း၊ abbreviated to ၎င်း၊ both—, and—, also.

လယ်ထမင်း၊ a rural feast; a picnic. (now obsolete.)

လိမ္မာ၊ to be clever.

လုပ်တိုင်း a burial ground; a grave.

လုလ္လ၊ (pron: လုံလ၊) diligence; industry.

လုလ္လင်၊ လုင်၊' (pron: နှလင်၊) a young man.

လေသာပေါက်၊ a window.

လောက၊ (Pali) this world, or existence.

———နီတိ၊ (Pali) a book of proverbs, pertaining to common life.

———ဘာသာ၊ (Pali) philosophy.

———ယတြာ၊ (Pali) magic.

———ဝိဒုဝိဋ္ဌာ၊ (Pali) logic.

လောဘ၊ (Pali) selfish desire, cupidity.

လိုက်နာ၊ to obey ; listen to.

လွင်ကျင်း၊ an open plain.

လှင်တန်၊ လှင်တံ၊ a rod, a stock.

လှည့်ပတ်၊ to go round, to deceive.

လျှောက်၊ to address (a superior,) to petition.

ဝ။

ဝတ္ထု၊ property ; a pattern, a representation, a tale.

ဝဋ်၊ (Pali) the evil consequences of sin.

ဝန်ခံ၊ to engage, to take the responsibility.

ဝန်တို၊ to be disobliging, irritable.

ဝမ်းမြောက်၊ to rejoice.

ဝိညာဏ်၊ ဝိညဉ်၊ (Pali) the soul.

ဖွက်ထား၊ to hide, conceal.

သ။

သင်းဂြိုဟ်၊ (pronounced သချိုး၊) to perform funeral rites.

သင့်၊ to be suitable, consistent, proper, befitting.

သင်းဂြိုဟ်၊ သင်းချိုင်း၊ a place for performing funeral rites, a burial ground, သုသာန်၊ လုတ်တိုင်း၊

သစ္စာ၊ (Pali) truth, veracity, faith.

သတ္တဝါ၊ (Pali သတ္တော၊) a rational being.

သတို့သား၊ သတို့သမီး၊ son, daughter, with the additional idea, of little, or dear.

သနား၊ to pity.

သဘင်၊ a festival, an assembly.

သဘော၊ nature, character, disposition.

သမ္ဘာဝိ၊ (Pali) steadiness in a good cause,—an honest person.

သမုဒ္ဒရာ၊ (Pali) the sea, ocean.

သံဝေဂ၊ (Pali) fear, particularly the fear of the consequences of sin in a future state.

———တရား၊ the law or doctraine of same.

သံသရာ၊ (Pali) the existence of any being, but particularly the future existence.

သာဓု၊ (Pali) well done.

သာယာ၊ pleasant.

သားမြေး၊ from သား၊ son; and မြေး၊ grand-son; e. g. offspring.

သိတင်းသုံး၊ to live, pass time,—applied to priests.

သုတ်သင်၊ to wipe, cleanse.

သုသံ၊ သုသာန်၊ see လုတ်တိုင်း၊ and သင်းပြွတ်၊

သုံးစား၊ to use, make use of.

သူ၊ a person.

———ကောင်းပြု၊ to assist, raise; said of kings.

———ခိုး၊ a thief.

———ငယ်၊ a boy, a youth.

———ငယ်မ၊ a girl.

———ဆင်းရဲ၊ a begger, a poor man.

———တပါး၊ an other person, others.

———တော်ကောင်း၊ an upright, conscientious person.

———မိုက်၊ a fool.

———သတ်၊ an executioner, a murderer.

သောတဝိညာဏ်၊ (Pali) from သောတ၊ the ear; and ဝိညာဏ်၊ the soul; e. g. hearing.

www.ingramcontent.com/pod-product-compliance
Lightning Source LLC
Chambersburg PA
CBHW021424090426
42742CB00009B/1242

* 9 7 8 3 3 3 7 3 7 4 2 1 1 *